Mind Your Own Business

A Nonfiction Book

by

Donald Akutagawa, Ph. D.
and
Terry Whitman, Ph. D.

Marian,

Thanks for making

my visit so pleasant

International Standard Book Number:
1-885487-00-2
Library of Congress Catalogue Card Number:
94-066620
Printed in the United States of America

Published in 1994 by

Brownell & Carroll, Inc. Publishers
3901 Mac Arthur Blvd. Suite 200
Newport Beach, California 92660
1-800-643-6604

Preface

Each of the chapters in the book is written from the viewpoint of one therapist, even though both authors wrote the material. The vignettes are composites of many cases, but are presented as single instances for readability.

Although there are many references to children and parents, this is not primarily a book about families. It is a book about *relationships*. Territoriality has such extensive applicability, that it applies to human beings of all ages and all manner of affiliations. The subject matter of this book covers a wide variety of interactions to illustrate the great breadth of application of the principles.

Acknowledgments

Any creative enterprise is a group project in the sense that it rests on the shoulders of all who have preceded and who made a contribution to the ideas that form the foundation. Our work owes its fruition to these predecessors as well as those we recognize and acknowledge below.

Robert Ardrey stands in the tradition of "translators" who have made some key scientific discoveries known to, and understandable to the rest of us. By making those ideas available, they have made it possible for us to solve some problems we might not otherwise be able to unravel. His *Territorial Imperative* gave us the initial understandings upon which we elaborate in this book. To him and to our many teachers and mentors, we owe more than we can describe.

Frank Sisko planted some of the first seeds that led to *Mind Your Own Business!* Our clients, colleagues, relatives and friends helped us to apply territorial concepts and discover how they worked.

Bringing those ideas into book form was due to the creativity and encouragement of many individuals. Mary Anne Mauermann, Linda Lee and Bette Hagman, besides their continuing encouragement, made crucial contributions to the clarity of expressions, but aren't responsible for the unclarities that remain. To our publisher, Jack C. Polley, who recognized the broad applicability of the concepts of territoriality to ordinary life problems, we owe our opportunity to bring the material before the public eye.

Table of Contents

Mind Your Own Business

Part 1: Territories and People

Most human difficulties center around territorial struggles. The issues involved can be complex, and most of us are unclear about what is our territory and its boundaries. Before we can "mind our own business," we will need to know what is ours to manage.

How an individual makes some of the first gains, and the natural consequences of it on other members of the family, are often problems between members of a family.

Intrusions into space claimed by others provokes defensive behavior in the tenants of the territory. The intrusions and the space involved can be quite different, but the reactions of those who claim ownership are always proprietary and defensive.

The kinds of territories for which individuals struggle can be quite different at different ages, but the process of gaining and losing territory continues through life.

Our protective reactions with our territories require that we identify our possessions. Sometimes we must use "fences" of various kinds, and the "stuff" of which those barriers are made is frequently anger. Skill in building and using such boundaries is necessary to minimize difficulties.

Part 2: Problems Between Parents and Children

This chapter focuses on conflict between two people as a private, shared territory. Intruders—parents in this case—are punished in various ways for violating this private domain. The solution comes only with recognition that the fight is a private matter, a "business" that belongs to the two who are in contention.

Aggressive harrassment and exploitation, when a weakness is evident as a pattern of behavior, isn't restricted to animals in the wild. The tenant of parent territory can also be a target.

Respect doesn't automatically attend the ownership of the role territory of "Parent." Not only must it be earned, it has to be required. The blending of love and anger in eliciting respect is much more powerful than either alone.

As a teenager struggles with the problems of his age and status, he discovers, with much pain, that he must come to terms with the broader society of which he is a member in order to enjoy the benefits of membership. He learns that one may "fight with City Hall," but probably can't beat it.

Without our clear awareness, we all sometimes give gifts with "strings attached," conditions under which the gift is granted. In essence, we share possession while expressing the idea that we are giving a gift. The consequences can be destructive.

Giving children too much help, guidance and protection can be damaging to children. Realistic parenting is hard for parents to do, but is necessary for healthy growth.

What might seem logical and practical as a defense against intruders may sometimes turn out to be worse than the problem we faced in the beginning. A common occurrence is depicted in this chapter.

A major hurdle for most individuals is to achieve parity in their relationship with their parents. Some parents won't allow it. But becoming a peer with one's parents—at least in one's own mind—is a necessary step in becoming a grownup.

Parents often have difficulty sharing the territory of their children with others, even with someone they've married. But if they don't, they create much difficulty. Respecting the conflict territory, owned by their own child and the other adult, is important in working out problems.

Part 3: Territorial Problems with Partners

Many couples take literally the dictum that "two shall become as one" and then engage in warfare trying to be the one who controls the couple. Resolution of their differences requires recognition that they must maintain their separate identities as well as share some functions at other times.

Conflict between parents over the role territory of "the dominant parent" can wreak havoc within the family and aggravate ordinary difficulties to the level of increasingly destructive events in the family. Resolution of their differences depends on the parents dividing the role domain, instead of having a "dominant parent" role.

Individuals in couples often fail to see that their own viewpoint is only one of myriad possibilities, and behave as if they had a "handle on truth." Their efforts are then directed to persuade their partners to "be reasonable" and see things their way. If they realize there are many realms of "truth," they have the possiblility of greater harmony between them.

This chapter focuses upon the truism that, as members

of a couple, we are often our own keepers—in the sense of jailers. When we recognize that we can be our own keepers, in a more constructive sense of being caretakers of our own self domains, we can be free of what we formerly experienced as shackles.

Old shoes are often more comfortable than new ones until the new are broken in. It's human to try to keep things the same, even though we feel limited by our ruts. Expanding horizons in life is interesting but can occasionally be frightening and uncomfortable.The conflict between comfort of the old and the challenges of the new sometimes creates problems between partners.

This chapter will advance a most unpopular notion: that personality differences can be irreconcilable obstacles, which limit the number of areas in which harmonious action can be taken. Only if those differences between individual territories are recognized, and accepted as relatively permanent characteristics, can the individuals remain together and have some semblance of harmony. In some cases, those differences result in breakup of the relationship, and the individuals blame each other for being stubborn and causing the rift.

This phenomenon is commonly confused with the garden variety of "falling in love," but is a vastly different experience. Only a few people are privileged—or doomed—to undergo it. It is an experience that is ten times as intense as ordinary involvements of a man and a woman. Few couplings can survive the rigors of it. Survival of the relationship requires uncommon clarity of the individuals' identity territories. The experience leaves residue that is valuable and durable.

Part 4: The Self Territory

become in an adult's life. The point is made that compliance with the former is necessary for socialization, but decision making is necessary for constructive adult living and for survival.

Although we are taught that we only have one emotion or motivation at a time, our motivation and emotionality is more often multiple. Most of the time, our emotional life takes a dual form: one for, one against. Duality of emotions is almost always present and is basic to inner conflict. Resolving inner conflicts requires a problem-solving, decision-making model.

This chapter will deal with the advantages, if not the necessity, for cultivation of the self territory. That requires discovery of the contents of it, then development and enhancement of the elements discovered, so one can live life most fully and satisfyingly. The alternative is not to live fully, and in later years to be regretful and unfulfilled.

This section is an overview of the basic ideas in human territorial behavior.

xiii

Introduction

"**M**ind your own business!" is an expression most of us have heard at one time or another—spoken to us, or by us. It is an aggressive rejection of one person's attempt to influence or to intrude into the affairs of another. The statement asserts ownership of the "business" in question.

Almost every problem we have with another human being is because we aren't clear whether we are dealing with "my turf," "your space," or "our place." In essence, we aren't always clear about what belongs to us, what belongs to the other person, and what is shared.

In the movie, *Never Cry Wolf,* both the hero and a wolf were shown marking the perimeters of their territories with urine. What they were doing is similar to fence building, outlining the limits of property and boundaries.

These fences, whether in human or wolf society, reduce the amount of conflicts individuals have with others of their kind, both from within the local group and from those outside the group. Outsiders, wolf or human, recognize such boundaries and rarely trespass on the territories so marked. If they dare enter, they are quickly routed by the residents. For the wolves, such markers and ownership have survival value as they reserve the right to a certain amount of available den space and food. For humans, equally vital needs are served by owning and holding territory.

The territories we own vary so much in their names, nature and dimensions that we are often confused about them. Among other names, our territories are called possessions, turf, domain, realm, property, belongings and our "business." Added to these are a variety of territories that we label as ours by saying, "my" or "our" space, area, rights, prerogatives, privacy, time, commitment, investment, etc.

The kinds of territories we own include not only physical objects and space, but also psychological entities as territories such as "my ideas," "my invention," or "my theories." We can consider certain relationships such as "my family," "my country," or "my friend" as our belongings. Certain priorities, such as "my turn," "you are next," are dealt with as possessions, too.

Territories and their boundaries are also subject to change, as for example, when we sell our homes and move, or we change our occupations, or increase our claims when as sales representatives, we gain new or larger territories.

Because most of us aren't clearly aware of the borders of our domains, ordinary happenings become unnecessarily complicated and destructive. That means we are all burdened—sometimes to the point of extreme stress—by difficulties we don't need to have.

We all have an intuitive grasp of territorial principles, but that isn't sufficient to use the principles effectively. The level of our knowledge about territoriality can be compared to knowing enough about cooking to fry eggs or a hamburger. We'd need much more knowledge and skill to bake a pie, or make Bouillabaisse and Crepes Suzettes. Likewise, in order to be able to use the principles of territoriality effectively, we need to be consciously aware of them, and to develop skill in using them.

Just as a plain piece of colored glass is enriched and made more interesting when we look at it through a kaleidoscope, looking at ordinary situations through the idea of territories will open up new vistas we hadn't realized were there to be seen.

Most psychiatrists, psychologists and other human behavior specialists seem to have regarded those ideas as too obvious or too simple to be of much use in their work. The authors, however, have found those ideas to have *very* practical and valuable use in their work with people in trouble. We will show in *Mind Your Own*

Business! how relevant territories are in our daily living, and how the application of their principles has beneficial use for us.

You, as a reader, will learn how to recognize where and how those principles operate and how you can utilize your awareness to solve many practical problems quickly and easily. Mainly, you will become much clearer about just what your territory—your "business"—is, and how you need to manage it to keep it under your control and avoid most unnecessary problems. Essentially, Mind Your Own Business! *is intended as a "User's Manual" of territorial principles.*

Part 1.

Territories and Persons

The major difference between human and animal territories is that while most animal territory is spatial in nature, human domains may be symbolic and psychological as well. That makes human territory and its boundaries very difficult to identify. As a result, we are often unaware of trespassing on others' holdings. And trespassers may intrude on our territories without their awareness or our knowing it. Our greater understanding of territoriality facilitates problem solving, because territories are involved in almost everything we do. But before those ideas can be useful to us, we need to know more about where, when and how those ideas apply.

In Part I, we will show how territorial principles can be used to solve many ordinary problems. Many of them start out as simple difficulties. The attempts we make to eliminate those difficulties often result in unnecessary aggravation so they then become problems. By viewing these problem situations through the "telescope" of bounded territories, we will find simple and effective solutions for many of them.

Chapter **1.**

)/(inding
)/(y Own ßusiness

- **A** young woman is cooking and her visiting mother offers a suggestion. The young woman suddenly gets a splitting headache.

- A mother wants her son to clean up his messy room. Within 30 seconds, they are in an old familiar argument that leads nowhere.

- Two young policemen enter the open door of a house where a man is assaulting a woman. When the officers try to break it up, one of them gets stabbed in the back by the woman they were trying to protect.

These three real life situations, while seemingly quite different, have in common disagreement about who has the right to do what, with which, and to whom. That type of disagreement is involved in every conflict between two antagonists — whether they be animals or human. *These are all territorial battles* — a struggle to be in control of a particular piece of business — and emotions aroused in such situations can reach murderous proportions.

When the boundary around a territory is clear, such as the walls of a house or a fence around a building, there's less conflict about ownership or control. But when the boundaries aren't clear, or there is dispute about who owns the "business," contention arises quickly.

In a recent television commercial for a headache remedy, a mother offered a suggestion to her married daughter, who was cooking. The daughter reacted by holding her head, with a pained expression on her face. "Mother, please! I want to do it myself!"

A parody of that ad in another TV program, showed the daughter taking a frying pan and hitting her mother on the head with it. The audience howled. Their reaction revealed their identification with the daughter's anger toward a meddling parent. But many parents must have been horrified by such antics.

In a different family fight, Jessica confessed that she and her ten-year-old son, Craig, often argued about whether his room was clean and neat.

Craig would protest, "But I just did clean up. Look at it. It's 1000 times better."

"It's still a mess. You haven't picked up your underwear from under the bed, a sock is still hanging from the lamp, and there's junk and dirt all over the floor."

"Well, isn't this *my room?*"

"Yes, but this is *my house.*"

The impasse they'd reached is only a way station on their endless journey toward the "Valley of the Happy Family."

In a third situation, a patrol car pulled up to a small home from which shouting and screaming could be heard. The officers entered the house through an open front door and separated a husband and a wife who were fighting. The man had a large welt on his face and the woman's nose was bleeding. One officer took the man into another room while his partner helped the woman stop her bleeding. All the while, both wife and husband shouted insults and obscenities at each other.

"You're not a man. You're a yellow, pot bellied, chicken livered coward who only fights with women and children!"

Her husband charged past the officer standing between him and his wife, screaming, "I'll kill you, you lousy bitch!" The two officers tackled him and one struggled to put handcuffs on him.

"You leave my husband alone!"

As she screamed at the officers, the woman picked up a butcher knife and stabbed one of them in the back.

When his partner was wounded the other officer drew his revolver to get the woman and her husband to back away so he could call for assistance. Although the couple's friction seems to end when the police van carts them away to jail, we know that is only a punctuation in an almost endless sentence.

Great differences can exist between people without their necessarily becoming a fight. The differences become conflict when two parties contend about who is "right" or who "owns" the territory. We all have difficulty with someone else because we don't have clear ideas about our territories, our "business" and its limits.

For example, our territories can be physical space. But if we are driving on a highway, how are we to define the space we regard as ours when it is traveling with us at 55 miles an hour? And when we say, "my family," "my company," or "my country," are we excluding the ownership of anyone else? Sometimes, yes.

And then, those physical spaces can change dimensions. Sometimes, when we ask someone to leave us alone, we might mean our physical bodies. At another time, we might mean the whole room in which we are working. And yet another time, we might mean, "Get out of my sight — forever."

But what kind of territory is "my business?" Or my political beliefs? Or my religion? And what is meant when someone says, "As the father in this family, I should have certain rights?" Are all these territories? Indeed they are. As humans, our territories aren't only physical space or objects. Sometimes the ownership struggle is over abstract "rights" or the roles we play.

We can tell when we are dealing with a territory when: we become angry with someone else or they are angry with us; one tries to get the other to do or not do some-

Minding My Own Business

5

thing; and there is a struggle, in words or in action, in which one is usually successful in driving the other away, or one submits to the other in some fashion.

Another way we discover that a territory is claimed is when we find someone acting possessively and defensively with it.

Jessica and Craig, her son, have some clarity about the territory they are struggling over: physical space. The problem is complicated by the fact that the space Craig is claiming is contained within the space Jessica claims. Their conflict ceases when Craig cleans up to his mother's satisfaction, or she retreats in resentful righteousness — until the next battle.

The police officers and the fighting couple are dealing with more complex territories: a private fight (which belongs to the two who are fighting), peacefulness of the neighborhood (a territory that is "owned" by the community), physical bodies (owned by the individuals), a private home (which might be owned by the couple), the laws (which themselves are rules about many public territories) and individual rights (governed by the laws of the broader community and which belong to every individual). There may be other kinds of territories as well which are involved.

The reason we aren't all fighting one another continually to win or control territories, is because there are rules governing ownership or control which most of us accept. It's only when we don't understand, don't agree about, or when we don't accept the rules that conflict occurs.

A few years ago in California, the newspapers reported a conflict between two families over an unfenced piece of ground that was two feet square in area. The battle took many forms, including the installation of floodlights, cutting down each other's shrubs at night, and squirting each other with garden hoses. Eventually, the issues had to be settled by a court. To outsiders, the situation might seem silly, but the two families were deadly serious.

Disagreements between smokers and nonsmokers get very bitter. Are they contending over the right to unpolluted air, the right to smoke, the right to control the behavior of another person or the right to make — or break — rules?

The fact is, most of us are often unclear *about what is ours to manage and what is not. And the more intimate a relationship, the less clarity there is likely to be. With those who are close to us, we share so much that we lose sight of what is "yours," what is "mine," and what is "ours." That's why so much conflict occurs between intimates.*

Besides the fact that some human territories are abstract, another factor makes for problems. Not all territories are clearly marked. Most human territories lack visible boundaries and markers to show someone owns them. And since we often aren't aware that we are trespassing, we are jolted when we are challenged by an owner. When we are aware that we are approaching space, issues or things that might be owned or claimed, we need to check into the matter.

Many of us look down on "small talk," thinking it is a stupid waste of time. But when we meet a stranger, that's how we start getting acquainted. There is a good reason for this. We are checking into territories and their boundaries. Small talk is a series of probes, to see if there is unmarked territory we may be entering. Instead of barging blindly into hazardous, owned turf, we gingerly explore.

But whether it is a marital squabble, sibling rivalry, a family fracas, quarreling lovers or a gangland battle over drug selling rights, the conflict rages about some kind of "territory" or "turf" and its possession. Before we can mind our own business and stay out of the affairs of others, we will need to know what is ours and what isn't. And before we attempt to take over some new territory, we will need to judge whether it is open to be possessed, if there are laws which regulate ownership, and how much opposition we are likely to meet.

In the next chapters, we will look at different kinds of territories and show how an understanding of territorial features helps to avoid unnecessary difficulties.

Mind Your Own Business!

Chapter 2.

First Gains

*A*cquiring territory is full of hazards and pain. But having some space we call our own is so important to all of us that we will risk pain — and sometimes even our lives — to win some. Some of the earliest struggles take place between a child and other members of the family and continue into adulthood. From these first experiences the degree of clarity or the depth of confusion about ownership learned at home, we carry into later life and situations.

Six-year-old Sheila and her sister, Darla, two years younger, seemed to be playing nicely until Darla decided she wanted the colorful toy Sheila held. Sheila physically protected her possession by giving Darla a push backwards, making her fall on her bottom. Darla's ear-piercing shriek brought her mother, Bertha, running to see what had happened. The mother suggested to Sheila that she should share with her little sister.

"But it's mine," she protested, "She's not supposed to grab my toys. She has her own."

Bertha explained to Darla that she mustn't snatch Sheila's things. Learning about ownership is a long and hard road that has many a tear-filled experience in it. All of us have trouble with it, throughout our lives, but most of such pain is avoidable. Darla, with a lot of unclarity about territorial rights typical of her age, had tried to take something that Sheila regarded as her territory. Sheila made an aggressive defense to keep control of the possession. In kind, her defense was no different than the wolves' which aggressively defend their geographical space from the efforts of outside wolves to take over.

From the first sense of possession, the "property" of a child progressively increases. At first, the possessions are food, toys, bits of fluff, or other objects, and the first pocket into which they are deposited is the child's mouth.

But as the child gains more and more territory, from where does it come?

From the holdings of other family members, to begin with.

Does that mean the child must engage in struggles with other family members to win territory? To be sure. But at early ages, when the child lacks knowledge, strength and wiles, the others are usually happy to give what the child needs and wants. If they don't, the result is a disaster for the child.

Some parents consulted with me about their four-year-old child, who wept a great deal, screamed, had fits of sleeplessness, and was so insecure, he had to be held and comforted all the time. I learned that the child was required to keep his room completely neat. Every toy had to be kept in its proper place. The room was spick and span. Every minute of the child's life was managed by the parents who required everything to be done "the right way."

What the child needed was some territory of his own that he could manage. He needed space he could call his own, toys he could play with when he chose and decisions he could make. He had been so closely supervised, he felt he had nothing to call his own, not even his own choices. His parents even tried to teach him to share his toys with other children before he had a sense of ownership. As the parents gradually learned about territoriality and let him have his rightful share, the child gradually calmed, lost his unhappy look, and began to play like a normal four-year-old.

Usually contests for control of territory, between parents and children start as early as when the child is two to three years of age and continue in some form until the child leaves home. The later struggles are to win the territory of decision-making rights.

When three-year-old Kevin found that, "I want . . ." didn't always work, he had some head-on confrontations with his mother. That didn't always work, either. Kevin, being a persistent and creative child, tried a series of other approaches. He tried crying, and then gave sulking a whirl. He stumbled on a surefire technique that worked with his mother, Shirley. He stuck out his lower lip, looked sad and looked on the verge of tears. That was too much. Shirley said, "O.K., but just this once." Kevin brightened immediately — which made her feeling of pity change into pleasure.

"Just this once," was of course only the beginning of a long line of "onces." Kevin had learned to play on his mother's sympathies, and later developed a whole battery of "poor me" techniques. In later life, he was able to manipulate many people into giving him territories of privilege, favors and concessions by using a skillful martyrdom. That worked well for him in getting more control over some areas of his life, but it also led to a sense of poor self esteem.

When I was a new graduate, I visited some friends who had a rambunctious five-year-old son, Steve, and a three-year-old daughter, Laura. Steve wrestled his sister to the floor while they were playing good-naturedly. Steve then lay on top of Laura and wouldn't let her up. Laura became upset, cried and screamed at Steve to let her go. Steve grinned and didn't move. I fully expected the parents to intercede, but they didn't. They continued their conversations with their guests.

Eventually, Steve let her get up, crying. Laura went to her father for comfort, and Steve went to play in another room.

A year later, during another visit at the same home, Laura was sliding down the stairs on her stomach. Steve approached her and tried to grab her feet and pull her down the rest of the stairs. Laura turned to face him, and drew her arm back ready to punch. Steve laughed and went on to other things. I realized then why her parents hadn't rescued her from Steve. She didn't need it. She had learned to fend for herself.

Beyond self defense, Laura had more clarity and appreciation of some of her own capacities and skills, as well as about her own courage and independence — all because her parents hadn't taken over her problems. Instead, they had left it up to her to find a solution.

For normal growth and development children need to make decisions and exercise choices. Most parents try to prevent their children from making mistakes — which is one of the most serious of territorial violations. All children need to be allowed to make mistakes. Errors are opportunities to learn. As parents, all we need to do with their conflicts is to protect them from dangerous or serious consequences.

One most important understanding all parents need is the recognition that as a child grows and needs more and more territory, the parents *must give up territories they have possessed.*

Although many parents easily give their children things and advantages they themselves never had, some parents give too much and resent the imbalance but aren't aware of it. That resentment often emerges indirectly. One form it takes is the demand that children repay them in absolute obedience or submission. Another is in the expectation that their children will be forever grateful and repeatedly tell their parents. In some cases, parents will arbitrarily refuse something to a child that could easily be given without depriving the parent.

While some parents can let their growing children have more and more territory of various kinds as their competence increases, other parents have much difficulty and trauma. The one territory that provides the greatest amount of difficulty is the right to make decisions. For normal growth, every individual needs to make as many decisions as competence allows.

Parents who aren't able to release control get into power struggles with their children. When the child is younger, of course, he has to give in. Later, in teenage years, it becomes a question of whose will shall prevail.

Most of these contests are verbal, but occasionally they become physical — and dangerous.

Jamie, at 16, spent a lot of time in the gym lifting weights. As a result, he developed a powerful physique.

One evening, his father ordered him to get out of a particular chair so he could sit down. Jamie didn't like the way he was being treated, and refused. His father went over to him and said, "You get out of that chair right now, or I'll knock your block off!"

Jamie didn't move.

His father pulled his arm back as if to throw a punch.

Jamie stood up. "Don't do it. I don't want to hit you."

"*You* don't want to hit *me*? You little punk!"

He started to swing. Jamie blocked the punch and landed one of his own squarely on his father's chin, knocking him flat on his back.

Without a backward look, Jamie grabbed his jacket and left. He never came back.

That kind of exchange is unusual, but it happens. Most parents are aware of the drastic things that can happen if anyone is cornered and desperate, so they don't push things that far. Some parents, like Jamie's father, are deceived by the fact that their children allow them more leeway for error than they will tolerate from outsiders. But there is a limit.

Territorial battles don't have to be serious or dangerous confrontations. They can also be playful and enjoyable.

Thirty-five years after that early confrontation between them, Sheila and Darla were together making preparations for a family reunion at Darla's home. Darla answered the phone, spoke for a few minutes and then hung up.

Sheila asked, "Who was it?"

Darla looked at her with mock indignation. "That's none of your business, Miss Nosey."

Sheila pursed her lips and shook her head. "Always the hard one."

"Well, if you must know, it was my friend LouAnn, asking when our club would be meeting."

"Oh. I thought it might be cousin Sue."

Those incidents between the sisters so many years apart

are quite similar. Both of them are territorial struggles. Although the roles were reversed, one person tries to get something the other person has. The possessor protects her possession and rejects the intrusive efforts of the other.

Even though the contexts, the people, their ages, the approaches and the defenses are different, the basic similarities when these situations are viewed through the "telescope" of territories help us to understand the rivals' reactions.

Regardless of how much territory each of us is able to win, there are always new spheres to conquer. As we grow from childhood into adulthood, our needs and interests change, and so do the kinds of gains we seek.

At the same time we try to win some new turf, we must be on guard to protect what we have, as there are others who seek it. We don't have to become paranoid about other people, but we do need to be alert to avoid serious invasions. But no matter how alert we are, we will lose as well as gain territory.

Chapter **3.**

Taking Over

When we consider taking possession of something, we should be aware that what we assume to be "free territory" may not be. As a matter of truth, there is little of that kind of property lying around to be taken over. Just because there are no territorial markers in sight, doesn't mean the territory isn't claimed.

Marla asked the young man sitting at the table in the library, "Is this seat taken?"

The young man looked up momentarily, and said, "No, I don't think so."

Marla pushed the newspaper on the table to one side and sat down. She was hardly into the second paragraph of her reading when she heard a somewhat irritated voice.

"I think you're sitting in my seat." A middle aged man in a business suit, loomed over her, resentment on his face.

"I didn't think anyone was sitting here."

"Well, you pushed my paper aside to sit down. You might have known the seat was taken."

Marla apologized and moved to another table.

She had mistaken the newspaper as "trash" rather than seeing it as a territorial marker. The person who thought he was leaving his reservation tag used something that is too easily seen as trash. A book, a pad of paper or a briefcase would have served better.

Although the above situation seems trivial in the scheme of life, it is one of countless unnecessary difficulties we face every day.

Marla had simply taken possession of space that didn't seem to be "owned" by anyone. She later regarded the man as a crusty codger who was a bit peculiar, and she was left with a twinge of discomfort. One of these incidents has little effect; ten thousand can place much strain on us.

In this interaction the businessman was establishing temporary ownership over what is generally recognized as public property. He was exercising "squatter's rights," a common, and generally accepted behavior. But he could have avoided his own irritation and Marla's experience of unpleasantness by leaving a more conspicuous marker.

Acquiring territory is always fraught with the risk that it is already owned. If we aren't aware of that possibility, we can get ourselves into a lot of unnecessary stress and strain.

A couple of mushroom hunters, foraging for their favorite fungus, were confronted by an angry man with a rifle.

"You're on my property. Drop those bags and get the hell out of here. Right now!"

Needless to say, the mushroom pickers left the scene, leaving the bags of mushrooms. They had crawled between strands of barbed wire fencing, intent on their task. Of course, they realized the fence was a boundary marker, but they hadn't anticipated they would run into the owner — and the aggressive defense he might put up. They returned from that foray into the woods emotionally troubled for weeks.

Violating boundaries is always a risky venture. Sometimes it results in such bruised feelings, but it can also end with severe injury or death.

Drug dealers or gangs who intrude into turf "owned" by other dealers, gangs or by the broader community often set off shooting wars. People are killed or wounded in these battles. That violence, and their invasion of public territory, quickly brings the police down on them. Criminals are clearly aware they are intruding, but they boldly challenge the tenants, as they are usually armed and aggressive. Regrettably, in many cases, they are able to stay and exploit the space they have taken over.

Victor, a man of 25, newly out of the service, decided to set up a grocery store in a poor neighborhood. His business was hardly two weeks old when he found graffiti spreading like a cancer from the other buildings to his newly painted front. His welcome for the third week of business was a visit by a local hoodlum who robbed him at gunpoint. He had worked hard establishing a business but was forced out in six months. Taking over space in that area was easy enough to do, but protecting his turf from being invaded and exploited by others was next to impossible.

In our history books, the colonial settlers are often portrayed as good people who only wanted to explore and settle into unowned spaces. Indians are depicted as savages who warred against those innocent people for no good reason. From the viewpoint of territoriality, those conflicts can now be seen differently. The settlers took what looked like "free territory." They could not have been aware the land was owned by anyone, as there were no territorial markers they recognized. The Indians, however, saw them as usurpers and fought for their holdings. The government now recognizes the priority of ownership in some cases by making cash settlements for land taken over from Indian tribes.

The term, respect, is relevant here. Respect means, "to look again." It implies some consideration before action. When we see an opportunity to move into something that looks like "free territory," it would be wise to look again. That doesn't necessarily mean we shouldn't move in, but only that we should be aware of what we are doing, and judging the risks as we go.

But simply because the territory is currently held by a tenant is no reason to avoid an attempt to take over. For instance, the holder of an athletic title can be challenged and displaced. Or a holder of political office can be a fair target for unseating. In business, the fact that one company dominates a particular market is all the more reason for competitors to move in and try to take over. Writers, entertainers and politicians are always attempting to take over an audience or a share of the public's attention that is being claimed or temporarily held by others. *At one time or another, we are all invaders of territories,* as we are trying to win something worth having. We may be opposed in our efforts, and it is necessary to be aware of that.

Territoriality has no moral position, no value stand. It is only a group of ideas for understanding some kinds of human behavior.

Chapter **4.**

Independence Odyssey

As our children progress through life, many of us worry that without our control and guidance, they will fail. We often underestimate their capacity to use good judgment and to cope.

Fifteen-year-old Tracey wondered, "Shall I tell my parents what I'm thinking of? No, they'd have a fit and try to stop me. I'll just do it, and not tell them. After it's done, they won't be able to do anything about it."

No, Tracey wasn't planning a bank robbery, or even a wild party. She was thinking of getting her ears pierced.

Her mother's reaction was just what she anticipated. "How could you? Why didn't you talk with me first? You can't just go off and do as you please about everything. You're getting too wild in your ideas, young lady."

There was further gnashing of teeth and some lecturing from her parents. The ear-piercing was only one of many things Tracey did that concerned her parents enough to come to me for consultation.

Her father said, "Children these days are getting wild. At fifteen, they're doing things I never even thought of when I was that age."

"At 15, I don't think Tracey is a child any longer. She's a

young woman." My comment was ignored by both parents.

"I wonder what's going to happen to her," her mother said. "If she just goes ahead and does as she pleases, there's no telling what she might do next. I really worry about her. She's so different from her sister, Allison. Allison never has given us the kinds of trouble Tracey has."

When I saw Tracey, she wasn't sure what she was going to encounter in coming to my office.

I said, "Your parents tell me you are having a lot of trouble with them. From your point of view, what seems to be happening ?"

"Not much. My parents get too excited about every little thing I do, as if it meant I was going down the tube."

"What do you mean, 'They get too excited'?"

"Well, like getting my ears pierced. After all, they're my ears, aren't they? My parents act as if that's a certain sign I'll end up as a criminal or a bag lady."

She rolled her eyes in disgust.

"They always think I'm going to get into some kind of big trouble. I've thought of doing something wild to fulfill their expectations, but I don't want the hassle."

"What's the worst thing you've ever done?"

She thought for a minute or so, then said, "I've skipped a few classes. I've been to a beer bust and drank a little beer — about a couple of teaspoons — because I don't like the stuff. A bunch of us went into one of the local department stores and shoplifted some cosmetics just to prove we could do it and get away with it. I guess the only other thing I've done that would horrify my parents is once, two friends who were sleeping over and I, sneaked out a window about two in the morning. We went to the math teacher's home and stole some plums from his trees."

These revelations, so easily shared, showed considerable trust that I wouldn't share the information with her parents. In our modern world, most teenagers know a good deal about privacy and confidentiality rules, but Tracey's sharing was also a reflection of her openness and awareness that her behavior was ordinary and common to her age group. She was clearly aware that her parents' views were very sharply opposed to such behavior.

Underlying the conflict over the pierced ears was a much more fundamental struggle. Tracey's mother was primarily concerned with the decision-making territory as the relevant issue, and she felt she should have control over that domain because she filled the role of "the mother," and that included supervision over most decisions. Clearly, Tracey disagreed.

Tracey, in accordance with her increasing age, was seizing control of more decision-making territory. Her mother was obviously uncomfortable about Tracey's having acted independently in this realm, and wanted to keep control over it. But more basic still, for this mother, was the special invisible bond between mother and daughter that seemed threatened.

In an interview with me, Tracey said, "I don't tell Mom and Dad that I've been to a "kegger," or that I've shop-lifted. They'd have a fit and bring me to see you or some other 'shrink,' thinking I was showing signs of emotional problems. Do you think I'm a mental case?"

"No, I don't think you're a 'mental case.' I think you and your parents are having some pretty normal problems of life. But I think you and your parents could do some things differently so you wouldn't have so many battles."

"Well, please help us do that, because I'm getting pretty tired of it."

In my next interview with her parents, we reached agreement that Tracey was maturing and that she needed to take over more and more decision-making. *But that understanding at the intellectual level didn't mean the struggle for control was ended. Emotional acceptance, as a primitive remnant of our animal beginnings, always lags behind agreement in the head.*

Her mother said, "But I'm afraid she'll make mistakes."

"She probably will. But most of them will be learning experiences for her. You only need to protect her from dangerous and serious consequences."

"That's what I'm trying to do. I don't want her to be a prostitute."

Such a highly specific worry can reflect serious conflicts in the parent, but they can also be stereotyped concerns of a different generation. In this case, they were expressions of the latter.

"I think you're underestimating your success as parents. You've actually succeeded very well in guiding Tracey so that she's accepted most of your values. She's an emotionally well functioning person, and she's becoming more independent every day."

"That's what I'm afraid of," her father injected.

"What is it that you worry about if she becomes more independent?"

"She may do something absolutely stupid."

"For example?"

"She could get arrested for something."

"And then?"

"Well, in a way, it would serve her right."

"What do you suppose would happen if she did get arrested?"

"I guess she'd learn a hard lesson."

"And you might not even have to say or do anything?"

Tracey's mother was uneasy about the direction our discussion was taking. She said, "But I don't want my daughter to have a police record."

"I'm sure you don't, but neither does Tracey. Tracey is a normal teenager. She's experimenting with greater independence, and she's likely to make some mistakes. *The most important things she, or anyone, needs to learn is that her choice was a mistake, and to take responsibility for having made the choice.* I can assure you that she does take responsibility for most of her choices — much more than most teenagers."

Because I had seen Tracey in two individual interviews by then, I had an opportunity to know quite a bit about her and her activities. I was sharing my conclusions about her without revealing the information she had given me.

"What Tracey needs most, now, is the opportunity to try her wings, and to learn from her mistakes. Her judgment is reasonably good, so she isn't likely to make really serious errors. But if you prevent her from having the natural pain that comes from goofing, it will take longer for her to learn."

Reluctantly, her parents were able to back off and allow Tracey more freedom to make decisions. The family tensions eased. Tracey was much happier, and the parents were more relieved that they didn't have to shoulder so much responsibility for her actions. We stopped our regularly scheduled appointments.

Two years later, Tracey and her parents were back in my office, unable to reach agreement about where she would go to college. Her mother wanted her to go to the state university in their city, and live at home. Tracey wanted to leave the state and go to a Midwestern college. Her father could see the merit of both sides, and didn't have a strong preference.

Tracey said, "I think mom wants me where she can keep an eye on me, to keep me from becoming a local criminal."

"Now, Tracey, you know that's not true. I think you need to make the transition to college in a more gradual way. If you do well, you can attend any school you want after that."

"Do *you* also need a gradual transition from having Tracey home, and having her halfway across the country?"

The tears started. Tracey moved over and put an arm around her mother's shoulders.

"It's not as if I were dead and gone, mom. I'll be back. I just don't want to live at home for two more years while I go to school. I need to go away and live my own life like a reasonably mature person. I don't need a mommy to hold my hand anymore."

"What do you have in mind, Tracey?" I asked.

"I want to go to a school in the Midwest. I have a chance for an athletic scholarship there. They have a championship volleyball team and think I could be a strong addition."

Her mother spoke, "But Tracey, that's so far away, you wouldn't be able to come home more than once or twice a year. And besides, there's more to life than playing volleyball. You could well afford to spend more time on your studies."

"Being away will be just what I need. I'll have a chance to make it on my own for a while, and not be your little girl. I'll never make the grades Allison does, but she'll never be the volleyball player I am."

Tracey did win her athletic scholarship and went to the Midwestern college of her choice.

Three years later, her mother called for an appointment. She entered my office looking very worried and several years older than I had remembered her.

"Well, I'm back again. This time it's very serious. Tracey's father doesn't agree with me that we should interfere, but I think we should do something.

"Tracey's in her Junior year. She's met a young man and thinks she's in love with him. From what she's told us about him, we think he's a playboy and a ne'er-do-well. She plans to drop out of school and marry him! I can't stand that. I'm so angry with her flightiness and unpredictability."

"What would you like to do?"

"I'm thinking of going out there to meet his parents and tell them what's happening and get them to put a stop to it."

"What do you suppose Tracey's reaction to that would be?"

"She's asked me to come out to meet him and his parents. But she doesn't know what I plan to do. What do you think?"

"I think it would damage your relationship with Tracey. She's a very independent young woman and I don't think she'll allow you to interfere with her life that way."

"I was afraid you'd say that. I guess you're right. I suppose I'll have to leave it up to her to make of her life what she will. But it just kills me to see her do such stupid things."

Tracey and her mother were still engaged in their competitive struggle. Tracey was seizing control of her decision-making rights as territory that belonged to her, and she had already demonstrated many times that she was effective in protecting those rights against several attempts by her mother to take control.

Of course, Tracey's mother was driven by more complex motivations than the competitiveness, but exploring that territory wasn't what I was being asked to do. I had probed earlier to see if she were amenable to dealing with her own underlying problems, and she had strongly indicated that she wasn't. One of the most powerful motivations was the loving bond and the special place Tracey had in her mother's heart.

I heard later that Tracey's mother had tried to persuade the two young people to wait until after graduation to marry. But Tracey dropped out of school and eloped with the young man.

Her mother came to see me a few months later. She said, "I just knew it wouldn't work out. Tracey's pregnant and her husband is out playing 'with the boys.' They don't have any money, and they're having a hard time. We've sent them money from time to time. I can't bear the thought of that baby being hungry!

"It's so hard to let Tracey live her own life. I know it's something I must do, but when I see her doing some of the things she's doing, I just have to try to get her to change direction."

She left, feeling more ready to cope, without intruding on Tracey's domain.

I saw her again, two months later. She was distraught.

"She's done it again. She kicked him out. She said she could do better without his problems. She's on welfare. I was going out there, but she said she wouldn't allow it. If I went to her residence, she said she wouldn't let me in. I know she means it."

Gradually, she was coming to accept the fact that Tracey would live her own life, and that her own upset and disturbance were her "business," her problems to deal with. She saw clearly that Tracey's apartment was her territory and she was capable of defending it against intrusions. Accepting the separateness was still difficult. Tracey was much clearer about her turf and its boundaries, and her clarity helped her parents to stick to their own responsibilities.

Tracey's father seemed resigned. He said, "I can't say I approve of some of the decisions she's made, but she hasn't complained to us or asked us to rescue her. She's been a regular trooper. She's had some hard times. I have to admire her pluck."

Having refreshed their perspectives and resolve, they left my office. As they did, Tracey's mother remarked, "I haven't even seen my little grand-daughter, and she's over a year old. We offered to send Tracey tickets to come out here, but she said she'd come when she could afford it."

Several more years were to pass before I heard from Tracey. A year after her divorce, she met Dave, a talented and promising physician. They married and seemed to do well. Some years later, Tracey's mother wrote me a note, saying that Tracey, David and Trisha would be visiting them.

When she arrived in town, Tracey called to see if she could see me for a few minutes. She came to my office with her husband, Dave. They presented the appearance of a conventional, middle class couple, well groomed and stylish. Trisha, Tracey's five-year-old, who appeared to be a well adjusted child, entered holding on to David's hand.

"I wanted to thank you for helping my parents and me. They grew and changed a lot, and so did I. You knew I had to be me and do my own things. I just wanted to tell you that I have appreciated what you did for us. You helped my parents to 'keep the faith.'

"And I wanted to let you know that I didn't end up on the streets as a 'bag lady.' I'm a sales rep for a high tech company, and am doing very well. With prize money that I won for being top salesperson of the year, David, Trisha and I are going to Denmark.

"And one other thing. We three are champs at minding our own business."

Chapter 5.

Anger And Fencing

When we try to define our territories, anger can be a necessary "fence," to maintain boundaries assertively and to protect our domains. If we don't use that anger, it may accumulate and remain as resentment. A collection of resentment becomes bitterness that can escape from control and become destructive.

Many of us have a misconception that time itself will take care of such feelings. But a simple test will demonstrate to us that may not be true. Think back upon an event long past which aroused great anger in you that you didn't resolve. As you go through the images of that time, you will find the emotions of the past in nearly the same force and color now.

Let's look at an example. Before consulting with me, Bradley was the kind of person who never forgot a trespass, but who would never confront a trespasser.

Bradley told his wife, Julie, that their neighbor was erecting a new fence between their homes. "I think Jon's building on our property."

"Why don't you talk to him?"

Although Bradley decided to say nothing, he became moody. He complained loudly and long to Julie.

After several frustrating sessions with him, Julie said, "I don't

27

want to hear any more about it. If you're only going to complain about it and do nothing, don't tell me about it anymore."

"But you're my wife."

She walked out of the room.

Bradley followed her and complained. She wasn't living up to her responsibilities as a wife. After ten minutes of pleas, shouting and, finally, tears, Julie started packing her bag.

"There's only one way you can stop me from leaving. That's for you to get on the horn and make an appointment with a marriage counselor for the two of us."

Bradley had resisted seeing a counselor many times before, saying that he was sure they could solve their own problems. Over a period of four years, they were making dismal progress. Reluctantly he agreed to make an appointment.

Once in my office, Julie took the initiative. "I've got a child on my hands. He only wants to cry on my shoulder about how mean the neighbor boy is treating him, but insists I go punch him."

"I only wanted to tell you how I feel."

"Sixteen times?"

"It wasn't 16 times."

"Bradley, I don't want to be your mommy anymore. I want you to grow up and be a man."

To get some specific details about Julie's charges, I asked, "Tell me what you mean."

"Our neighbor is building a fence and Bradley thinks it's being built on our property. He's angry, but he won't talk with Jon about it. He's complaining like a little child, telling me the same things over and over. I'm fed up with it. I don't care if Jon builds a fence across our living room. I don't want to hear another thing about it."

"What does the situation look like from your point of view, Bradley?"

Obviously embarrassed by his wife's outburst, he took a few seconds to gather composure.

"I've been thinking of talking to Jon."

Julie gave him a withering glance.

"Well, I have. But Jon and I never did get along, and I want to be sure to handle it so things will get better, not worse."

Bradley tried to ignore an audible snort from Julie.

"Have you thought of what you might do?"

He thought for a moment. "As a matter of fact, I have. I'm going to call my attorney tomorrow, and see what he would suggest. Then, I'll call Jon and tell him I want to talk to him."

Julie couldn't suppress a giggle. "This, I have to see."

I ignored Julie's comment. "That sounds reasonable."

Bradley did call his attorney, who advised him to have the property lines resurveyed, so that he would be sure an error was or wasn't being made.

It turned out that Jon's fence was seven inches over his legal property line. Bradley then went to talk with Jon.

"Hi, Jon, I wonder if I could talk to you."

"You mean about your surveyor who was here last week? Well, I've hired a surveyor of my own. I don't take anyone else's word for anything." He went on with his work without looking up.

Bradley retreated.

Jon's surveyor confirmed the location of the property line where the other surveyor had placed it. Resentfully, Jon moved his fence to conform with the legal requirements.

Bradley was fortunate that both surveyors agreed on the property lines. Had Jon not called in his own surveyor, the tensions between him and Bradley might have gotten considerably worse. Although his relationship with Jon didn't become better as a consequence of those events, that was the price Bradley paid for taking necessary action. If he hadn't, the cost might have been very much greater.

For example, he would have had to cope with continuing resentment about what was, in essence, usurpation of some of his territory. He would also have suffered a loss of some self esteem and self doubt, in having allowed it to happen. Then there would be increased apprehension that Jon or someone else could do a similar thing to him again. Saving more and more anger would eventually reach a stage where it could properly be called "hate." These consequences would persist and add to a general store of tension with which he would have to live.

Although there are some people who think all situations can be managed with sweetness and light, more realistically, some can't. Protecting our privacy from invasion will sometimes require assertive, and sometimes angry, defensive action.

When our Far West was being settled, cattlemen began branding their cattle and building barbed wire fences as a way of keeping their cattle under control, and to protect them from rustlers. Today, we use the same techniques to safeguard some of our possessions. Instead of barbed wire, we may use a variety of boundary protectors.

Our next example shows how emotional "fences" can be erected for protection.

While co-workers Martha and Louise chatted in a small restaurant, a woman at the next table injected a few comments into their conversation. Martha and Louise exchanged knowing glances and continued on with their conversation as if they hadn't heard anything. They created a fence of disregard.

Later, at work, they were discussing business problems, when a young man, who had recently joined the company interrupted a similar conversation.

Martha turned and said quietly, "Jordy, we're having a private discussion and we'd prefer that you not intrude without being invited. If you have something to say to one or the other of us, please arrange to talk with us after we finish what we're doing."

On two other occasions, he did the same thing, not listening to Martha's quiet messages.

The next time, Martha was very firm, and clearly irritated. "Jordy, stay out of our private conversations. I don't want to talk to you anymore about this. You're a very rude young man with very bad manners."

Here, Martha increased her firmness and the directness of her message. Jordy heard the message and changed his flippant manner with them. "Keep off the grass" messages hadn't worked. Only when he ran into verbal barbed wire did he quit barging into Martha's conversations.

Most people don't realize that in human interactions, we need to gauge the forcefulness of our messages relative to the situation. When we use too much energy for the situation, we will feel guilty for doing more damage than was necessary. And if we use too little energy, the consequence is ineffective and frustrating. Learning to use the right amount of energy and the best form in sending the messages takes considerable practice.

If we want to protect our territory, we will have to learn to use many kinds of fencing, whether it is softly verbal, legally authoritative, cold repulsion or forceful anger and aggression.

Part 2.

Territorial
Problems In
Families

All of us have had dealings with members of families — our own or those from other clans. And in those dealings, with children or adults, we have encountered many territorial problems, whether or not we recognized them as such. In Part II, we will explore a variety of them.

Chapter 6.

Private Fight

In animal groups, one individual usually emerges as the leader, and that status is won through physical conflict. Relative peace reigns until struggle breaks out when a lesser member becomes bold enough to challenge the leader. Each time the leadership issue is settled, peace and order return, and each time that issue is unsettled, conflict and disorder break out in the group. With humans, physical conflict is more rare. The contests are usually verbal, but the pattern is the same. Peace and order are disrupted by every disturbance of the dominance order.

Long before he entered the kitchen where his mother was cooking, ten-year-old Davey's shrill screams announced his coming.

"Billy hit me! And I wasn't doing anything."

Marie turned down the heat on the pot, wiped her hands and strode down the hall to the Rec room. There sat the 12-year-old culprit, innocently watching a television program.

"Now, why did you hit Davey?"

"Well, he kept turning the dial to another channel when I was watching this one."

"That's no reason to hit him. You could have come and told me."

"Yeah, and you'd just tell me to share the television and let him change it to whatever he wants to watch."

"You're the older. You have to teach your younger brother how to share. You can share, can't you? Now you let Davey watch for a while."

The suddenly red-faced Billy screeched, "See? I told you so! You always take his side. It's not fair!"

Marie tried to calm him and persuade him to do what she wanted.

Billy glared in hatred, and his voice took on a deadly tone, "Just you wait. I'll get you!"

"Mom! He's going to hit me again when you leave. Make him get out of here. You have to make him stop."

Marie sent Billy to his room, crying in angry protest, "I hate him! I hate you! I hate you both!"

Marie despised such scenes, but she knew if she left Billy in the same room with Davey, he would carry out his threat, ruining the rest of the day.

This kind of event is ordinary, but it is an unnecessary misery that many families live through. The solution is very simple, but most parents are reluctant to carry out the necessary actions. What is required is that the two siblings be permitted to resolve their own disputes.

Before we get into solution details, we need to see what the nature of the problems is. We need to see what the territories are and to whom they belong.

One territory is the right to choose the television channel. That's the domain the two boys were struggling to win. Billy won the first round by sheer force. But Davey was successful in getting the alliance of his mother and in achieving control over the selection rights in the second round. His victory, however, isn't without some complication and future hazard.

Another territory is the fight itself, an interaction started by the two boys and, in a sense, "owned" by both — a shared territory. When Marie, responding to Davey's invitation, maneuver or manipulation, entered the conflict, she thought she was merely reacting to a plea for help from her younger child. *She did so without awareness that she was intruding into a social process "owned" by the two people,* and only one had invited her. Davey welcomed her intrusion. Billy resented it.

If we use the analogy of a partnership owned by two people, and one of them invited a third party into the partnership, we can readily see the complications. The third party might be invited and sanctioned by one of them, but since the partnership belongs fully as much to the other partner, he would, of course, resent the action and take steps to stop it.

But Billy, being a child, felt helpless to change what had been done, and lost the power to manage the TV choices.

Later, Billy, intruding into Davey's territory, "accidentally" broke one of Davey's favorite toys. While Marie comforted Davey, Billy's father, Phil, scolded, "Billy, you know you have no right to touch Davey's things."

"I was just moving it out of the way and it fell. It was an accident, it wasn't my fault."

These family squabbles are frequent. The more the parents try to mediate the problems, the worse they get. Billy was seen by both his parents as the troublemaker. But no matter how often he was punished, he continued to pick on Davey. Davey had to be rescued time and again.

What Marie and Phil didn't see was the clever way Davey could get them to take his side against Billy. They also didn't recognize that Billy's territories were being invaded and abused by the younger child.

One day, while Billy was watching television, Davey threw his shoe and hit Billy on the back of the head. There was no physical damage, but the assault on his body territory and memories of past incidents awakened a violent rage. Davey raced to his mother and hid behind her, smiling in glee at the raging maniac who wanted to tear him apart. Marie ordered Billy to go to his room until he calmed down.

"But he hit me with his shoe! You have to do something. He doesn't have any right to hit me when I wasn't doing anything."

Marie had to take Billy by the arm and half drag him to his room. All the way, the boy screamed at the top of his voice.

Billy, after a long series of losing battles, harbored a growing store of resentment, and his anger emerged in devious ways. Not only did he "accidentally" break things, he frequently justified his parents' rebukes by tormenting Davey.

Billy found that picking on Davey satisfied some of his anger, but also upset and frustrated both parents. He was, in effect, punishing them for interfering and taking his brother's side against him. His apparent accidental breakage of his brother's possessions was in retaliation for what he experienced as assaults on his rights.

This pattern of conflict management is widely practiced by parents who want to treat their children "fairly" by preventing an older or stronger child from dominating a smaller or younger one. But the long term results lead to exactly the opposite, as far as the children are concerned, and have consequences for the other members of the family.

Davey was learning to torment his brother and to manipulate his parents into an alliance with him against Billy. Both parents were experiencing feelings of guilt and inadequacy, feeling that they were failing but not realizing why or how. And Billy was collecting a progressively larger store of resentment, and was beginning to show his disturbance at school and in the community.

Billy's teacher reported to the parents that their son's grades had fallen off, his homework was sloppy, late or not done, and he was fighting on the playground. The school psychologist recommended they consult with a family therapist. Billy's parents, although very troubled, thought they could handle their own problems without the aid of an outsider — who would be expensive anyway.

Both parents put in more effort to get Billy to stop his bad behavior. They punished him, made him stay home after school instead of going out to play, and lectured him at great length. They supervised his homework, and sat with him many hours to be sure he did it. When he "forgot" to take the finished assignments to school, they reminded him or took it to school for him. The burdens of parenthood are many, but for these parents, they added many more by taking over much of Billy's territory: responsibility for his schoolwork.

They arranged with the teacher to have notes brought home by Billy, reporting on his behavior each day, and whether he'd brought his homework to class. Predictably, many notes were "lost," so that the teacher had to send them by mail. Billy even intercepted some of those notes and destroyed them before his parents came home. Meanwhile, his behavior progressively worsened.

The event that convinced the parents they couldn't solve the problems by themselves was the day Marie received a call from the security officer of a local department store.

The officer on the phone said, "Ma'am, your son was caught taking some perfume from a counter. We'll make out a report to the police department and you'll have to pay the store a penalty of $200 for the offense. He's sitting here in the security office, and we'd like you to come down to get him."

Marie was devastated. She had visions of her son becoming a criminal. She felt ill. After a call to Phil, they decided that he would take off from work and bring Billy home.

In my office, the parents related the story of Billy's shoplifting. That type of behavior was completely out of character for either of the parents' families. We reached agreement for them to be seen in therapy. They were surprised that Davey would be involved as well.

In the first interview, as the family members entered the office, Davey and Billy saw that one of the chairs was on a swivel. They both raced to get it. Billy easily pushed Davey aside and sat down. Davey whined, "See, Billy always gets his way." Both parents tried to persuade Billy to let Davey have the chair. Billy, sensing that he had an advantage in a public situation with a stranger present, defied them and insisted that he was there first.

That first encounter supplied a lot of grist for the therapeutic mill.

I addressed the parents, "Apparently the two of you seemed to think you needed to correct something here."

Marie answered, "It isn't fair for Billy to take advantage of his size and dominate Davey."

"So you were trying to make it fair?"

"Yes," Phil said, "if we didn't, Davey would always come out on the short end."

"So when you both join in with Davey against Billy, that makes it more fair?"

The parents seemed uncomfortable with the question.

Phil volunteered, "We don't want Billy to lord it over Davey."

I rephrased my question to emphasize its importance, "Are you saying that three against one is fairer than for the bigger boy to dominate?"

"I hadn't looked at it that way," Phil said.

Billy, seeing his advantage, chimed in, "Yeah, they always take Davey's side and that's not fair. I always have to give in."

"When that happens, how do you feel, Billy?"

"I get mad."

"And what do you do with the mad feeling?"

Billy looked at his parents to see what their reaction and attitude was. Apparently deciding to be bold, he said, "Then I pick on Davey — but I don't start it all the time. Sometimes he starts it."

"It sounds like you're saying that *both of you* are responsible for the fighting."

He agreed.

"Do you sometimes start the fights, Davey?"

"Sometimes." His voice was very soft, almost as if he didn't want his parents to hear him.

"Then it seems to me that you two guys should settle the fight by yourselves. You have a right to have problems with each other, but it's not fair for you to make so much of a fuss that you bother your parents with it. Maybe you should fight outside, so you won't drive your parents crazy, and so they won't have to interfere in your fight. What do you think?"

Billy's face lit up in eager anticipation, "Yeah."

Davey said, "But then Billy would hit me and hurt me."

"Yes, I guess that could happen. But I hope you wouldn't hit him too hard, would you, Billy?"

Obviously enjoying this turn of events, Billy smiled as he shook his head to show his agreement.

Both *boys were responsible for their difficulties, and both parents were guilty of intruding into a private fight. By intruding into, and managing the* conflict territory, *they were effectively preventing the two boys from solving their own problems.*

Beyond that, without realizing it, their attempts to resolve issues and to make things fair were actually making the problems worse. By taking Davey's side, they were giving him an advantage, so that he could be bolder and provoke Billy. That would accomplish several things: it would allow him to get back at his brother, it would provoke Billy to be angry with him and maybe even start a fight, and that could result in more support from his parents.

Marie and Phil said that the most important consideration in dealing with their children was that they should be happy individuals. They, like many parents, got lost in their view of what their proper parenting task was. The primary task isn't to make children happy, necessarily, but to help them become competent to function in life. And part of that competence is to learn to deal with life's problems on one's own. If they are happy in the process, that's an additional plus.

Our knowledge about territoriality has helped us to see that one very primitive pattern of behavior leads to much better solutions than Marie and Phil were using. That pattern is the "the peck order." It is an organizing process that works as effectively for humans as it does for animals.

With great reluctance and difficulty, Marie and Phil agreed that the next time the two boys were in a battle, they'd require both of them to take their conflict outside. They had a right to the territory of their squabble, but they didn't have a right to inflict the disturbance on their parents' domain of peace and quiet.

Marie and Phil informed their sons what they intended to do. Davey protested, "But Billy will hurt me!"

Marie said, "That's going to have to be *your* problem. You two will have to find some way to get along."

Billy grinned with anticipation. But his parents warned

him that they weren't giving him license to commit mayhem. He had to be reasonable in what he did. No blood, and no broken teeth.

Shortly after, at home, the opportunity arose to test their new approach, as a loud argument broke out.

Phil said, "O.K., If you guys want to fight, you're going to have to go outside. You don't have any right to drive us crazy with your fighting. You go out and don't come back until you're finished fighting."

He made them put on their jackets and go outside. As soon as they were outside, they started laughing. "We're through fighting."

They were in the house for no more than two minutes when they renewed the battle.

Phil made them leave again. "This time," he said as he locked the door, "*I'll* decide when you're through fighting."

The boys hung around the doorway for a while, then disappeared. They returned together, two hours later, apparently in a good mood. They spent the afternoon in congenial play with each other. For two more days, the truce lasted. Then, another argument began.

Marie said, "Sounds to me like you two are getting ready to leave again."

The argument stopped.

When the boys got into an argument another time, Marie again made them leave. Outside, Billy wrestled Davey to the ground and lay on top of him. Davey screamed for help. Marie steeled herself and went into another room where she couldn't hear him.

In a few minutes, Davey came running to his mother in tears. "Billy wouldn't let me get up. And he hurt me. You've got to do something."

"Davey, I don't want to hear about your fights. You and Billy are going to have to find some way to get along."

On another day, Davey came to her with another complaint about his brother. Marie told him, "Sounds like you are having trouble with Billy. Why are you telling me?"

"You have to make him stop. He's always picking on me."

42

"But why are you telling *me*?"

She repeated the question each time Davey tried to tell her about the problem. In exasperation, he said, "Why do you keep saying that?"

"Davey, when you have fights with Billy, that's *your* problem. You're going to have to work it out with Billy, not me." Marie was sorely tempted to save Davey, but she was determined to see what would happen with the new approach.

A few weeks later, the once chronic difficulties between the two boys had diminished to a minimum. Keeping it under control needed only a reminder that they might have to take their fight outside. Contrary to the parents' expectations, Billy didn't continue to lord it over Davey. As a matter of fact, they managed much better and often played together, something they had done very little of before.

Davey learned to be humble against stronger aggressors, or to deal with them in good humor to defuse contention. He found that there are more ways to win peace than to defeat an opponent. Billy now had less reason to be angry with Davey, and discovered the rewards of leadership and the admiration of his brother.

Chapter **7.**

In Sickness And In Health

Animals in the wild will attack one of their number if they observe elements suggesting weakness or difference. Humans do the same. Any animal or human different enough from the norm becomes a focus of aggression and anger. The territories of individuals at a disadvantage, too, often become targets for invasion.

Mavis, in bed with the flu, had reached the end of her patience. She shouted at her 10-year-old son, "Get out of here right now and go to your room and don't come back for the rest of the day!"

Brian scooted from the bedroom where Mavis lay, feverish, exhausted — leaving her now guilty and depressed.

The next week, still recovering from her bout with the flu, she recalled her temper outburst. "I felt so awful, shouting at Brian like that, but he is a little Piranha, sometimes."

"How do you mean?"

"He picks a time when I'm not feeling well to get at me. He nips at me with his harassing, nagging and demands. No matter how I explain to him that I'm not feeling well, and even if I beg him to leave me alone, he won't stop. In fact, he does it more. He's like a jackal pouncing on a wounded animal, tearing me down. I used to think he was angry with me for not being available to help, but it's more than that. And he won't quit until I get so fed up that I scream at him. When he sees there's life in the old gal yet, he backs off to see if I'll get weak again."

Mavis' view of Brian's behavior represents one that many mothers describe when they aren't feeling up to par. Her description of Brian as a jackal with wounded prey has some validity to it. A primitive element in human beings seems to emerge at such times.

Although civilization veneers us with a coat of compassion, sensitivity and nurturance, many primitive tendencies remain seething beneath. Most of us don't like to admit that we have such components in our makeup but they exist nevertheless.

Mavis said, "I hate to think so, but I often wonder if Brian has some kind of serious personality problem, a sadistic streak in him. When I'm ill, upset about something, or just tired, he comes at me. I know it's true because I've paid special attention to it. I mean, it's not merely that, because I'm not up to par, he *seems* difficult. He *is* difficult."

"There's no doubt that he can be difficult. After all, he's a healthy, normal boy. Can you think of a reason why anyone — not just a 10-year-old boy, but anyone — would choose a time of weakness in another person to try to get something?"

"Well, from the way you ask the question, it's obvious. You're more likely to get what you want, then."

"A wolf will harass a wounded deer for the same reason. He's more likely to satisfy his needs there than with a strong, healthy animal."

"Are you saying Brian's behavior is the same as the high pressure salesman who browbeats a timid customer into buying his wares?"

"And the same as a person in a Las Vegas casino who's just won a few coins from a slot machine. If it 'pays off,' he'll try again."

She looked relieved.

"So you're telling me that I'm going to have to toughen up and tolerate that kind of behavior?"

"Not necessarily 'tolerate' it. You may understand why he does what he does, but you will still have to find some way to deal with it so you and he come out of the problem better."

"The only way I can think of to deal with him is to shout at him. He seems to hear me only when I get angry and yell."

"Or that's the only time he thinks you mean business."

"But I don't want to yell at him all the time."

"When you deal with him, you seem to go from one extreme to another."

"What do you mean?"

"You're either overly nice, understanding and gentle with him, or you angrily shout at him. What if you did something in between?"

"Like what?"

"Like being firm with him to let him know you mean it, instead of being patient and pleading with him. When you beg him to go away and leave you alone, you're telling him you're wounded and vulnerable."

"So even if I'm feeling terrible, I have to muster up enough energy to let him know I won't tolerate his hassling?"

"Unless you want him to continue."

Some months later, Mavis came back to deal with a different problem. She said, "Incidentally, that problem I had with Brian worked out beautifully."

"How did you do it?"

"One day, I wasn't feeling well and went to bed with a splitting headache. Brian came home from school, saw me in bed and started on me. I got up, took him firmly by the arm and escorted him to his room. I told him he was to stay there until dinner time, and that if he ever bothered me again when I wasn't feeling well, I'd keep him there until I felt better.

"Another time, I was exhausted. The minute he started on me, I told him firmly that it sounded to me like he wanted to get restricted to his room until I felt better. He quietly went to his room, and I haven't had any of the those problems since."

Mavis learned to use another tool besides the two she'd tried before without success. *She was cultivating her skills and knowledge, which gave her more power to deal with many different kinds of problems, and to protect her self territory from abuse.*

Chapter **8.**

Loving Anger

*M*any of us have difficulty dealing with our anger, as we would like to be seen as only benevolent, caring people. Because we separate anger from caring, the problem remains. What we need to do is learn to use both emotions at the same time in dealing with ourselves and others so that we can be angry and *loving.* When we do, we will find many additional benefits as well.

Marie had always tried to be kind and understanding with her son, Mark. Her approach seemed to pay off until she began to have trouble with him when he became sixteen.

One evening, she served a tuna fish casserole for dinner. Mark sneered as he looked at the dinner. "What's this supposed to be?"

Marie's stomach tightened. "It's tuna casserole, the kind you've always liked."

"I've never liked it. I'm not going to eat this crap! Get me something fit to eat."

She made several suggestions, which he rejected until she found a small steak in back of the meat compartment. While it was cooking, he drummed on the table with his fingers. When it was ready, he gulped it down, with mouth-filling bites, got up from the table and went out the door, slamming it behind him.

As Marie described the scene, she looked very sad and tired.

I asked, "How long has this kind of behavior been going on?"

"Since two years after his father walked out of our lives. Mark was ten then. Yes, it started when he was twelve."

"So this kind of thing has been happening for four years?"

"It seems much longer than that. Life's now so different from what it was. I get sick to my stomach when I think about it. Mark and I had been so close and he was such a joy. And now he's always stormy, hurtful and angry.

"I was delighted when Mark was born. He was a cuddlebunny who nestled in my arms and clung to me. I'd come from a family of 'touchers' but my husband, Len, was distant and aloof. I longed to be touched, so Mark was a wish come true. "Mark's father and I never did agree on much of anything, and we had many arguments about how to deal with Mark. I remember repeatedly hearing Len swearing at Mark when he was about seven. Then the sound of a slap, and Mark's crying. I'd rush in, hug Mark protectively, and say some angry, harsh things to Len. Of course, that led into more arguments."

It was only later that Marie learned in her counseling that she had intruded into Len's and Mark's relationship territory. At the time, she was aware only of much discomfort about Len's severity, and had jumped in to protect *her* son.

Mark was the center of Marie's world, her adorable little angel. They were inseparable. The love she'd wanted to give to a man, which Len couldn't accept, she poured on Mark. She was vaguely aware that it might be too much, but her loneliness was too powerful. She overindulged him, catered to him and made no demands on him. She cushioned his every hardship and sacrificed her own well-being for him, justifying it all by telling herself that no one could be loved too much. She was wrong. What she didn't realize at the time was that her closeness with Mark blocked his further development later.

"Len's and my relationship became more and more tense. After a while, we hardly talked to each other. One night, after an argument, he packed his clothes and left. I made no protest and even felt a sense of relief. He never came back."

Two years after their divorce, when Mark was twelve, her little angel turned into a devil. His once docile and gentle character became mean and spiteful. His bedroom became a mess, his manners abominable. He would "accidentally" break his toys or her treasured belongings. Her patience and forgiveness only seemed to worsen his behavior. No matter what she did, he continued to get worse. She began to feel he hated her, even though she didn't really believe that.

What Marie didn't see then was the meaning of Mark's behavior. His violation of her territory of treasured belongings was in retaliation for what he experienced as a violation of his identity and sphere of control.

When she brought Mark to see me, she thought surely she must be responsible for the change. She was right. But her part in it was very different from what she expected.

I told her, "Some of Mark's behavior is normal limits' testing. But another important segment comes from a natural and healthy part of him that needs to break away from his dependence on you. The two of you are too close. You're like two persons in one body. Mark has to get away so he can develop into a separate person."

Mark, like all children, intuitively knew he had to separate from the joint identity territory he had shared with his mother, and had to establish one of his own. Because Marie was clinging and trying to reestablish the closeness she once had with him, he had to fight all the harder to escape from her orbit.

Marie was crushed. She'd tried so hard. "Do you mean that, by doing so much for him, I've harmed him?"

"No, perhaps delayed, but not harmed him. His development has only been slowed. He can make that up easily.

"What concerns me as much as Mark, is you. You have devoted so much attention and care to Mark that you haven't taken care of yourself. What do you plan to do with your life when Mark leaves?"

"*Leaves*? I hadn't thought of that."

She was silent and thoughtful for several minutes.

That was the beginning of new directions in two people's separate lives. I helped her to recognize how she had neglected her own needs. At the same time I encouraged her to find ways to foster Mark's independence. *Like many women in our culture, she had become a very good slave, serving the needs of others without at the same time making sure that she got a fair share of life's goodies. This eventually made her feel so unworthy that, if anyone complimented her, she felt uncomfortable and denied she merited it. She was full of insecurities. No matter how much she did, she never felt it was enough. The self esteem of a slave, even though the slavery is in large measure self imposed, can only be a depleted one.*

And, despite her abundant love and good intentions, she was falling short in preparing Mark for life.

In essence, Mark was taking on part of her responsibility in provoking separation from her. Her excessive patience and understanding were failures to promote his natural separation. He had to work twice as hard when she wasn't doing her part. His obnoxious behavior was exaggerated by that need. And because he had to behave so abominably to get some emotional distance between them, he'd saddled himself with a sense of guilt. If he continued to behave that way, he would become a serious behavior problem and acquire some unnecessary emotional conflict baggage.

I told her she would have to "fight" with Mark. That wasn't anything like the things she'd read in the child care books and magazines. Her fighting, though, would have to be of a particular kind. It would have to set firm limits and it would have to be guided by a certain amount of self interest. But, instead of being serious antagonisms, the "fights" would be ways of giving Mark some space to develop his own identity territory. The best kinds of those struggles are "fun fights."

Dealing with Mark more realistically required of her that she treat him no better than she treated herself.

I told her, *"Only if you require it, will Mark learn to treat you with consideration and respect. The most effective way of setting limits with young people is to deprive them of your* services. There's very little that you can force them to do, but you can win their cooperation and help them to make wise choices that way."

She learned to deal with Mark differently. They had many aggressive confrontations.

Marie said, "I know that if some people could see and hear us during our loudest fights, they'd think us crazy. I have become quite good at playing the role of an angry, stubborn parent. It's against my nature to behave that way but I've found, through a lot of trials, that a snappy repartee is often the only thing that works for Mark and me."

She forced him to take over some of the domestic work. Cursing at her resulted in his walking home from school in the rain. He discovered that, if he broke something, his allowance was reduced until it was paid for. When he was rude, he lost the privilege of driving her car. When he refused to do some ordinary chores, such as mowing the lawn, he found he had to do his own laundry and ironing. Complaining about the "crap" she cooked permitted him to learn to cook many of his own meals. Refusing to do favors for her was followed by her refusal to loan him money or give him rides. A hidden benefit to all this was that Mark developed some competence in a lot of new areas of his life.

One week, he insisted on going out late at night. When Marie insisted that he stay in, he shouted at her, "You can't stop me from going out!"

She consciously made her voice calm. "No, but I can sure stop you from coming back."

For a moment, he debated within, wondering whether to challenge her further. Then he slammed one fist into the palm of the other hand and stomped off into his bedroom.

Today, Mark has become a courteous, friendly and happy young man, no longer the mean, resentful and selfish kid. He's learned to be a fairly decent cook and prepares dinner for the two of them when Marie has to work late. He's learned how to do his own laundry, can sew a little, and knows how to vacuum a rug and shop for groceries.

What Marie learned is, as Dr. Bruno Bettelheim wrote,

53

Love Is Not Enough. Our children also need our firmness, our power to deprive and coerce them occasionally, and the use of a sometimes-hard-to-achieve, loving anger. Answering his outbursts with righteous anger of her own became as much a part of Marie's behavior with Mark as her tender, loving care.

As Marie learned to take care of her own needs, she learned some valuable lessons.

She said, *"I had once thought that, if a person missed out on something, that was it. They'd have to do without it from then on. I've discovered that isn't necessarily true. As a child, I missed out on a lot of loving parenting. I've found when I treat myself in a loving, fair way, I feel loved and lovable. When I treat myself as a person who deserves respect and consideration, and require such treatment from others, I have good self esteem, self confidence, and feel energetic and full of life. Not only am I my own best friend, I can mother myself in some crucial ways."*

The result? She and Mark are both happier and *both know the limits and potentials of their identity territories.*

Chapter **9.**

Why Do I Have To?

*I*n some aspects of life, we all have to do the equivalent of "reinventing the wheel," going through the same experience to learn an age-old truth. One of these experiences is rediscovering that we can't always have things the way we would like, and that we can be overruled by more powerful authority.

Sixteen-year-old Scott discovered this when he was told to lower the TV volume.

"Why do I have to?"

His sleepy-eyed parents wanted to go back to sleep at two o'clock in the morning. "Because you have it on so loud you're waking everybody up."

"Well, big deal! You can sleep. Just ignore it. I have a right to watch TV if I want to."

"Not when you disturb other people. Now you can turn it off, or I'll remove the TV permanently."

"You can't do that. You don't have a right to stop me."

The next day, his father sold the television set.

Scott felt abused. He hadn't realized that he and his parents shared the family territory, and they were claiming the domain of a right to quiet during certain hours.

A different type of confrontation occurred on the other side of town. Two young men had a sophisticated marijuana growing operation in an underground chamber, outfitted with tanks, lamps, heaters and the necessary packaging supplies.

The police raided their operation and arrested the two. The marijuana was destroyed, and the equipment dismantled and wrecked. The young men were sentenced to prison.

Probably the young men were aware that they shared in the group's territory and its benefits, and underestimated the power of the community group, but they were challenging its authority by their actions.

In a third situation, Dana, a young man of 29, started to light a cigarette. Louise, an older woman in her fifties, asked, "Would you mind not smoking in this area? You're the only smoker in the office and the smoke bothers the rest of us."

"I like to smoke, and you don't have a right to tell me I can't."

"I'm not telling you, you can't smoke. I'm just asking you not to do it in here, because it pollutes our air."

Dana lit up anyway.

Here, Dana is aware only of his own territory, and resents what seems to him an outsider telling him what he can or cannot do in it. He apparently didn't hear Louise's remark, or chose to ignore it, as she very clearly told him that she was dealing with the group territory of air free of cigarette smoke and not his personal turf.

That afternoon, in a special meeting called by the owner of the company, they reached agreement on a policy not to allow smoking in the area where they worked. Dana was told he would have to smoke outside in the hallway. He wasn't happy, but he went along with the ruling, as he recognized the group had the power to enforce its decision.

These three situations deal with a problem that all of us confront from time to time. It's a question of "How much can I be me and do what I want, and how much must I go along with the group?"

The answer can be different for each individual and for

each situation but, in most cases, a group can defeat an individual. Each group will have different rules and, in most cases, we have choice about whether we will stay in the group or leave it. If we stay, we must conform to many demands of the group, or they can punish us in some way. It is much harder — almost impossible — to leave some groups, such as the culture or the nation. Besides, if we left one group, we would quickly find ourselves in another — with different rules that might be even more difficult to accept.

Scott was a determined young man, convinced that he could do as he pleased and no one had the power to make him behave. He didn't accept what he was told by others; he had to find his own answers.

Scott's father told him, "In order to share in the benefits of my work group, I have to conform to some basic rules, too."

"Yeah, yeah. Spare me the lecture."

"Just listen to me. If I want my job, I have to do certain things to keep it. Otherwise, I don't get to keep its 'perks,' including the use of the company car."

Scott didn't want to hear any more. He walked out while his father was still talking.

He still had some way to go to be convinced.

Later, he had a confrontation with a different group. He received a ticket for speeding. He raged to his father, "I was only going ten miles over the limit. Why isn't the cop chasing criminals instead of stopping me for a minor thing? I have the right to drive any way I want."

"You could," his father said, "but the law could take your driving privileges away."

"I have a right to drive. They can't stop me."

"I don't think that's accurate. Driving is a *privilege* we can have as long as we follow the rules. They can take the license away anytime for good reason."

Scott was still convinced he could do as he pleased. He began to test his version of reality. He got three more tickets and his license was suspended. When he continued to drive without a license, he was eventually arrested for that.

His mother said, "When are you going to learn? Don't you realize you're headed for serious trouble?"

Scott said, "I don't have to put up with this crap! I'll get my own place and do what I want."

His parents agreed that was a good idea.

Scott had little idea how he would be able to finance his own way, but he got a job and found two acquaintances who were renting a small apartment, and who offered to share it with him. Scott failed to pay his share of the rent, and one day found his belongings on the deck, with the lock changed. He had to move on. He was discovering the hard way that, if he didn't comply with the rules of the group, he would lose the right to share in the group's territorial advantages.

Scott was determined to drive, with or without a license. He went to auto dealers, telling them he was interested in buying a car, but wanted to test drive them first. He found that he could take joyrides with brand new cars, doing so at several car dealers, until they got wise and stopped it.

He next dabbled in stealing cars. He "hot wired" cars he liked and wanted to drive. He got away with it several times, but was then arrested and put on probation. That didn't stop him. He continued his new venture until he was arrested again. This time, he was detained in a center for delinquent youth for ten days.

Unconvinced that he could be forced to do anything, or that he could be stopped from doing as he pleased, he walked away from detention and left town. He was apprehended for auto theft two months later, and returned to serve jail time of one month. When he was released, he was again arrested driving a stolen car, and was jailed again, for 60 days.

After his release, he again left town, which violated the terms of his probation. It took another seven months before he was again picked up for theft. He received a sentence of six months of jail time, but was released on probation for good behavior.

Scott was a determined young man, but he wasn't stupid. He was now convinced that his course of action was only leading to more and more trouble for himself and, while he could get away with violating the rules from time to time, the odds were he would eventually have to pay the piper. He gave up his budding criminal career and has stayed within the limits of the law since that time. He still isn't a stickler about conformity, but he knows the practical reasons for complying.

He is beginning to be aware of territories and boundaries — his own and those of the groups. He is also coming to appreciate the power of the groups to enforce their requirements.

Scott had a hard time in the outside world, because he hadn't learned some basic lessons about territories at home. His parents told him about rules, but didn't adequately enforce them. As a result, Scott became a skilled manipulator, and defied their rules until their desperation drove them to back up their talk with action.

To join with anyone else, we necessarily give up some of our individual freedoms. But in exchange, we gain some benefits. It is a tradeoff.

Chapter **10.**

Gifts With Strings Attached

There is an old trick that was foisted on the unwary. A wallet, or something that seems to be of value, is left on a sidewalk where passersby can see it. Attached to the wallet is a near invisible string. When someone tries to pick up the object, it is pulled out of reach by the prankster. What seemed to be a valuable find, turns out to be empty air. Some gifts are like that.

Although he wasn't aware of it, David, the father of 18-year-old Brian, was the perpetrator of such a hoax. An upstanding citizen, and a person admired by his friends, David was embarrassed to learn about his role in the hoax when he came to see me about the problems he and Brian were having.

He said, "I've tried to be a good role model for my son. I've tried to live as a good example, to demonstrate to Brian those qualities which will bring him success if he'll only follow it.

"Brian has a good head on his shoulders. He knows right from wrong and he would never do anything to hurt anybody, and that's what puzzles me. Everything he's doing right now is counterproductive."

"Everything?" I asked, gently challenging his measure of his son's actions.

"Well, no. Not everything — it just feels like it."

"What specifically has he done that is upsetting to you?"

"I guess it boils down to only two things, but they're contrary to any of the values I've modeled for him. First, there's the issue with his car, and secondly, his telephone bills."

"Tell me about the telephone bills."

"Over the summer, he's accumulated over $700 in telephone bills. I can't believe it."

"Are the debts on your telephone account?"

"Yes, and each month after the bill arrived, I sat down with him and explained to him that I couldn't afford his bills."

"And how did he respond?"

"He was always apologetic and he sounded sincere in his intent to control his calls."

"Was he responsible in any way for making payments?"

"No, he doesn't have a steady job. He has tried a few jobs over the summer, but he hasn't stayed with any job long enough to make much money."

"Why not?"

"Brian's a very bright kid and the jobs he took weren't challenging enough. He tried delivering pizza, working at a restaurant, and a couple of other jobs, but they just didn't hold his interest."

David was unknowingly creating problems for himself and his son, but accepting his role in Brian's overspending was not yet obvious to him.

"You also mentioned a problem about his car. Tell me about that."

"Brian had an old 'beater,' that was nothing but headaches for him. It was always in and out of the shop with mechanical problems. What little money he was making from his part-time jobs was going right into his car and so he was having trouble staying ahead of his expenses."

David's tone was apologetic, almost remorseful. In addition to being industrious, he was also sensitive and compassionate. His love for his son was evident in the feelings behind his words.

"I ended up giving him my car, and I bought a new one. I could afford the car payments better than he could afford the mechanic's bills. And the car I gave him *was* in tip-top shape."

"Was?"

"That's what irks me so much. The car I gave him was immaculate, but he has abused it. He hasn't done anything to care for it. One of the fenders is dented, the upholstery has been stained and the car hasn't been washed in months."

"So you gave him something of value in the hope of sparing him the expense and hardships that went with his old car?"

"I guess I didn't want him to go through all of the hardships I went through when I was his age. I was lucky to survive Viet Nam and to put myself through college."

"You wanted to give him the head start you never had?"

"That's right. I feel as if I've always been playing 'catch up,' struggling to make it to the top."

"Did you value the car you gave him?"

"Yes, I loved that car."

"Why?"

He paused and thought for a moment. "It was the first new car I ever had. All of my others had been used cars. I liked having a new car, the smell of the new upholstery and the shine of its finish. It meant a lot to me, and so I put a great deal of effort into keeping it clean."

"Did you also put money into it?"

"Well, sure. My car payments, the insurance, and the maintenance were substantial."

"If you hadn't put the money into the car, would you have spent it on other things, like vacations or clothes for yourself?"

"Yes, but I wanted the car more than those other things."

"So you were willing to sacrifice certain pleasures or possessions in favor of something you valued more?"

"That's right, but what has that to do with Brian?"

"You came to appreciate your car because of your past experiences of doing without. In a sense you had 'paid your dues.' What dues has Brian paid?"

Again, David dropped into silent thought. After a time, he said, "I see your point. Brian doesn't know what it's like to go without a car, and he doesn't have a sense of having earned it or having suffered inconvenience for it. It doesn't mean the same thing to him as it did to me."

As a parent, David had overestimated the importance of modeling. It is important but it isn't sufficient. We can demonstrate how to care for our possessions, as well as our loved ones, but children rarely take "ownership" of such territories until they experience some personal investment of effort in them. Without the effort there is little commitment to, and even less satisfaction in the use of the territory.

David's past had taught him that advancement, both in college and business, was based largely on effort. His initiative to put forth the effort came from his prior hardships.

With further counseling, David realized his role in Brian's irresponsibility. He came to see that Brian behaved as he did, partly because he had no personal investment in the car or the telephone. *Providing things for Brian and making things easy for him were only promoting his lack of appreciation for the things, and for his own talents.*

Brian felt resentful about what seemed, to him, his father's lack of respect for his capacity to endure hardship and his ability to cope with and overcome it. But beyond that, Brian resented the "strings attached" to his father's gifts. The car was Brian's only when he used it in a way that was acceptable to his father. There was no true transfer of the territory, even though David had signed over the title of the car. David had given his son only conditional ownership of the car. It was Brian's only with the unstated provision that he care for it with the same degree of concern that David had.

David's understanding of gifts with strings attached was heightened by his own experience with his parents. His mother had given him a family heirloom, a fine, large, handmade cherry chest of drawers that had been in her family for generations. Although it didn't fit in with the decor of his modern home, David dutifully put the chest in a prominent area of display, knowing that his mother expected it and would be deeply hurt if he did anything else with it. He said, "I guess I can understand Brian's feelings somewhat better when I think about that. The chest doesn't mean to me what it means to my mother. If it were left up to me, I would sell or give it away to someone who would appreciate it properly and give it a home of which she might approve. But, since I don't want to hurt her feelings, I keep it in my home. "And," he said laughing, "of course, I'm not wrecking it like some people I know might do."

Although his resentment about the gift with strings attached was much less than Brian's, he truly saw the justification for Brian's feelings and his actions. David's acceptance of the conditional ownership was a voluntary and considered one, based on his loving relationship with his mother, whereas Brian's, because of his immaturity, was a seductively irresistible one.

All of us resent unstated conditional ownership as it infringes on our independence. If we don't see clearly that we are accepting overlapping ownership, and that the decision is ours to make, we can resent what seems to be an imposition on our autonomy. Brian resented the bondage of his father's gifts because of the obligations involved. Being a young man, he was not yet able to understand clearly that acceptance of a desirable gift could result in some surrender of his freedoms, or in guilt aroused by disappointing his parent.

David resolved to deal with Brian more constructively and realistically, even though it might conflict with his tender feelings about his son. He saw that a good relationship with his son was more valuable than the limited partnership in possessions, so he stopped his lecturing, sarcasm and advice.

Of course, Brian continued to misuse the car. It eventually broke down in a theater parking lot. The car was towed away and Brian had to sign the title for the car over to the tow truck company as compensation for their undesired services.

David paid the telephone bills in order to protect his credit rating. He told Brian that, because he paid the $700 bill, there wasn't enough left in the budget that year to buy him Christmas and birthday presents. To David's surprise,

Brian didn't object. He seemed to respect the fairness of his father's decision.

Through their turmoil, Brian and David established their territorial boundary lines with greater clarity. David learned to stay out of Brian's turf, letting him solve his personal difficulties and to benefit from the drive and perseverance that hardship can breed. Brian also became better at keeping his father out of his domains. He was less willing to ask for or to accept gifts from his father.

Transferring or acquiring proprietorship of a territory is seldom free of conflict. Disputes like Brian's and David's inevitably arise unless both parties are very clear as to ownership of the turf. Skirmishes continue until it is clarified.

Chapter *11.*

Destructive Help

*E*ntering privately held space without permission can be rude and an invasion of someone's rights. Adults who suffer such intrusions can sometimes make their displeasure known or take effective action to protect their territories, but children are less able to do so. Usually, they have to discover subtle and devious means.

Ten-year-old Freddie dawdled at his desk. His father asked, "What's the matter, can't you do your homework?"

"No. I don't understand my arithmetic lesson."

"Here, let me help you."

His father sat down beside him and worked the first problem, explaining the steps as he did them.

"Do you understand now?"

"I'm not sure. Could you show me again?"

The father completed another problem, then a third. By the time he finished the sixth problem, he was visibly frustrated and angry. He surrendered in disgust, and told Freddie's mother, "I really worry about that stupid kid. I've explained the process to him over and over and he never gets it."

Meanwhile, the "stupid kid" had six homework problems done without lifting a finger.

This same sequence of events happened many times over a

period of three years. Freddie demonstrated, in a series of special tests, that he understood the arithmetic principles very well, and could work problems at an advanced level!

In this instance, Freddie *seemed* to need aid. But his reactions to the assistance offered nullified or rejected it, and he appeared adequate after all. Seemingly, he neither needed nor wanted the help. He wanted to deal with his own problem — his own territory — by himself.

An interesting consequence of the events is that the helper proved to be the ineffective one. This is a most curious result: The person who seems to be competent offers aid to someone who appears to be inadequate, but the tables are turned so that the competence issue is reversed!

Freddie's father barged in to help without being asked. He was entering the territory of problem solution without asking if the owner of the problem wanted help. In essence, he was violating Freddie's boundaries and assuming he would be welcome. He was effectively routed and punished.

Many parents who do what Freddie's father did, wouldn't agree that they were minding their child's business and might have to encounter the problems many times before they could be convinced they couldn't help. Parents can teach their children many things, but most children regard their schoolwork as belonging to them and their teacher. The intrusion of parents is usually resented by the child but, if the parents insist on helping, what can the child do?

The usual outcome of parents' intrusion into the realm of homework is poorer performance and decreased motivation to achieve in school. Because children are fearful of opposing their parents' pressures openly, they do so by passive-aggressive resistance. They "forget," "don't understand," or they have to have repeated explanations to which they fail to pay attention. In the case of some parents, the help they think the child needs is forced on the child, and the results are predictably negative and destructive.

The pattern with Freddie and his parents progressed further. In the fourth grade, Freddie had been a good pupil, but the next year his marks began to fall. His father was alarmed and "helped" his son even more. He supervised his homework, checked it to see that it was right and reminded Freddie to take it to school. But still, Freddie managed to forget it, so his father had to take it to school for him. Sometimes, Freddie would remember to take the homework but, somehow, it would get lost on the way. His father spent many hours working with Freddie on the homework. Freddie's mother joined in and the help extended to other areas. In spite of all they did, his marks grew progressively worse.

Freddie received rides to school, and was picked up by his mother after classes. He got instruction and advice on every area of his life. His merest whim was given immediate attention. He became the primary focus of family concern.

In high school, Freddie stole something from a store and was caught. His father hired an expensive lawyer and made sure his son suffered no consequence. Whenever Freddie was in any kind of difficulty whatsoever, his parents rescued him. Thus even his right to the natural consequences of his choices was taken away.

In one of the rare times that Freddie saw a counselor, he confided, "My parents want to run everything. If that's what they want, I'll go along with it, but I'll make them pay for it."

The sad part of it is that the whole family "paid" for it, including Freddie.

Thirty years later, Freddie, a forty-year-old bachelor, was still at home with his parents. He had a special role in the family: the "tolerated darling." His parents had tried to get him to go out and get a job, as other young men his age, but he couldn't seem to find one he liked.

Freddie's comments help us to understand his situation when he described his parents' help as "running things." He described their violation of his territories. But, because they were so effective in running his affairs, he felt unable to fend them off. The form his vengeance took is the subtle, but powerful, influence he exerted over them: chronic failure and a debilitating dependency.

At this time in Freddie's life, his parents would have preferred him to have an independent life but they still harbored needs to keep control over him. Although Freddie would have liked the independence his parents wanted for him, he also had great fear about being able to function on his own. But, more importantly, his vengeful needs were too satisfying to give up.

From the time we were very young children, many of us were taught to be helpful. It was part of the Golden Rule. If we expected others to extend a helping hand to us, we were told we should first be ready to help them. Complications, as those above, however, sometimes arise.

Freddie's history helps us to see how help can be destructive. Too much help is an intrusion into our domains, interfering with the development of our own competence and personal autonomy. If all our needs are met, there is less need for us to struggle. And the less we struggle, the less we develop the skills, attitudes and knowledge necessary for competence.

Too much "chicken soup" or "TLC" is poison to the growth and development of a young person.

Chapter **12.**

₣ortress or
₱rison?

Have you ever discovered one of your attempted solutions to a problem presented more difficulties than your original predicament? Sometimes this happens when we try to protect one of our territories, whether it be money, energy or time.

When Barlow, a bachelor of 34, came to see me, he didn't seem clear about what brought him. He confessed, "I haven't much energy, so I don't seem to be interested in anything any more. I spend most of my time watching television."

Barlow had held a variety of jobs, painter, mechanic, boilermaker, stevedore, clerk in an auto supply store, taxicab driver and carpenter. In each job he did well, which encouraged his bosses to offer him a more responsible position. At that, he either refused the promotions, or left for another job.

"What do you do in your spare time?" I asked.

"You mean, besides television? Not much, I guess. Every six months or so, I go see my mother."

"Why is that?"

"I think mother is disappointed with me. I never seem to do things the way she wants them done."

"For example?"

"Well, I've been doing some repair work on her rental houses, and she says I paid too much for materials and supplies. I should have looked around to see if I couldn't get them cheaper. I got some good deals, but she thought I could have done better. She said I didn't care about her and how much it cost her."

"Is she paying you for your work?"

"Pay? No, she says I should be glad to help my own mother."

"Are you?"

"Am I glad to help her? Yeah, I guess so."

"You don't sound very convincing."

"Well, I really don't mind doing some work for her, most of the time."

"Do you mind doing it *some* of the time?"

"When I have other things to do, I'd rather not."

"What do you do then?"

"I tell her I have something else to do, but she cries and says I don't care about her. To make her feel better, I do what she wants."

Through questioning, I learned his widowed mother was in good physical health, was financially well-to-do and that she got a large sum of money from his father's life insurance several years ago. She had made several good investments and owned some rental homes. Apparently she was very shrewd about money matters — and skilled in manipulating Barlow to do a lot of work, at little expense to her.

"How do you feel when she cries and you do work so she will feel better?" I asked.

"I think it's all right then."

"No. I asked you how you *feel* then."

"Well, I don't mind it."

"Now, you're telling me how you *don't* feel. I'm asking you what you *do* feel."

"I think it's O.K."

"Now, instead of telling me how you *feel*, you're telling me what you *think*. Thinking takes place in the head. Feelings take place in the gut."

With great difficulty and many repetitions of similar dialogues, Barlow eventually recognized his emotional reactions, and the difference between his thoughts and feelings.

In one of our interviews, I asked him, "How do you feel when your mother criticizes the purchases of material and the way you've done the work on her houses?"

"I'm not sure."

"You know where your feelings are?"

"Yes. By now, I'm fairly clear that my thoughts happen in my head, and my feelings are around my stomach somewhere."

"When you think about your mother's criticisms, what kind of feelings do you have in your belly?"

After some struggle, he said, "Not good."

"Again, you're telling me what you *don't* feel. I want to know what you *do* feel. Is it a pleasant or unpleasant feeling?"

A long pause.

"Unpleasant."

"Can you give it a name?"

He couldn't.

It took this kind of tedious and painstaking exploration for Barlow to become acquainted with an ordinary process taking place in his body, which he'd formerly ignored. Many people have such difficulties, especially men. Those who have much more awareness of their internal workings find it difficult to understand why some people have this problem.

In time, Barlow was able to identify this emotion of anger, which can be of different "sizes" and take a variety of forms. He was aware when he felt strong anger, but had difficulty recognizing weaker amounts of it. He learned to discriminate powerful degrees of anger, such as *rage or fury,* from lesser intensities of it in the form of *irritation* or *aggravation.*

The next thing he learned was the difference between the ongoing experience of *anger* and the stored form, or *resentment.* He learned that, when resentment is present in greater amount, it is called *bitterness*, and more than that is known as *hate,*

With this kind of preparation, he was ready to dig at the core of his problems with his mother.

"So, what feelings do you have about your mother's complaints?"

"I guess I resent them. I'm trying to do my best for her and all I get is criticism."

"What do you do with the resentment?"

"I don't want to hurt her feelings."

"So what do you do with it?"

"I keep it to myself."

"And then what happens to it?"

"It just goes away."

"But what if you think of all the things that made you angry in the first place?"

"I try to forget them."

"But the feelings are still there?"

"Yes, I suppose so."

"And you keep adding more. So now you have a large collection of resentment that you've been carrying around for years."

"I guess that's true."

"Have you any idea what happens to all that bitterness?"

He shook his head.

"If you don't use that energy for something, it becomes depression."

Somehow, that didn't surprise him.

In the following weeks, when he came in depressed, I asked, "What are you resentful about?" Our explorations often elicited significant information and he began to suffer less from depressive periods.

In a later interview, Barlow asked, "So now that I know I resent the way my mother deals with me, what can I do about it?"

"Tell me about a specific thing she's done that makes you angry."

"When I told her today I couldn't do some work for her because I had planned a fishing trip, she said I was being selfish and that I don't love her.

"Is it true?"

"No, I do love her. . . and I do get angry with her," he added hastily, smiling at his own awareness.

"So, what are you going to do?"

"I'm going fishing with my friend, because we've

had the trip planned for a month. I feel guilty, but I'm going."

"What is it you feel guilty about?"

"Hurting her."

"How are you hurting her?"

"By not doing what she wants."

"How does your going fishing instead of doing her bidding *hurt* her?"

"Well, if you put it that way, I guess I'm not actually *hurting* her."

"Doesn't your mother have a right to feel hurt or disappointed without you minding her business?"

"Sure."

"And if she chose to be happy or not even care if you didn't do some work for her, is that your business?"

"I guess not."

"Your business is the decision *you make. Your mother's reaction to your decision is* her *business."*

With this exchange, Barlow became more clear about what was his business to manage, and what wasn't. He was beginning to become emancipated, but he had a long way to go.

In a next interview, he said, "My mother still calls me and cries on the phone. I don't know what to do. Last night, she was on the phone for over an hour. I felt so awful, I wished I were dead."

"Or that *she* was?"

"Oh, no. I wouldn't want that."

"You've never wished you could be rid of the problems you have with your mother?"

"Yeah, I have wanted that."

"Have you ever worried about her?"

"All the time."

"A lot?"

"Yes, a lot. She's not young anymore, and I've worried that she might get hit by a truck while she's crossing the street. I worry about her getting sick or getting lost."

"Lost? You mean disappearing?

"Yes."

"When people worry a lot about something happening to other people, it often expresses a wish."

"That's horrible!"

"Just wishing things won't make them come true."

That was the beginning of Barlow's learning that the anger he "stuffed" didn't disappear. It leaked out in the form of excessive worries. As he came to recognize his anger, he learned to accept it as a natural part of his being human. Feeling anger was ordinary. How he used that anger could be constructive or destructive.

Barlow began to take charge of his own life more. With difficulty, he had come to recognize that how he lived his life was his responsibility — his territory. He played with the task of refusing to do some things for his mother when they weren't urgent and when they interfered with his own plans. He actively avoided her as he became more realistic about doing or not doing things for her.

In one interview, he said, "I've decided to get a telephone answering machine. That way, I can screen Mother's calls."

Later, he was troubled about this.

"I didn't talk to mother for quite a while, so she got a cab and came over to my apartment. I didn't answer her knock, but I think she knew I was home. After she left, I felt awful. She lives a few blocks away, so I was afraid she might watch me, and know for sure I was avoiding her. I started staying in my apartment more and more, and only went out after dark. It's been a miserable time, not being able to come and go as I did before."

"So the fortress you built to protect your own privacy became a prison for you?"

"Yes. Now, I'm my own jailer."

"Well, if that's so, you should have a key."

In his next interview, he seemed happier.

"I thought about what you said about my having a 'key.' I realized I was only hiding from the problem and not dealing with it. I decided I'd have to face the problem — my mother — and deal with her.

"She was mad when I admitted I hadn't answered her knock at my door. I told her I hadn't been honest with her and that I wanted to deal with her like a grownup. *From then on, I would do some things for her, but if it took a lot of time, I would have to charge her for my time just like any professional she would hire. I also told her that there would be times I would be unavailable to her. I had other things in my life I wanted to do. She was very upset, but she listened. My knees were shaking, but the more I talked, the calmer I became. And when I left, I felt happier and more confident than I've felt in a long time.* You're right. There are better ways to protect my freedom than locking myself in a prison."

There are times in all our lives when we need some kind of armor to protect ourselves but, ideally, that protection needs to contribute to our freedom or preserve what we have, rather than deprive or harm us.

Mind Your Own Business!

Chapter **13.**

Peers

An *important hallmark of our progress as adults is the way we* *deal with our parents. In a physical sense we may be mature, but* *many of us remain children to our parents instead of having our* *own identity territories.*

Katy, 29, divorced for three years, had been sharing her apartment with Fred for six months. She worried about the forthcoming visit by her parents. They were coming 2000 miles across the country for their first visit with her since her divorce.

In her first interview with me, she said, "I thought of asking Fred to move out temporarily, while my parents were here, but that didn't seem fair. Then I thought I'd tell my parents some kind of story, like I had to leave town, asking them to postpone their visit, but that didn't sit well with me."

"In your heart of hearts, what would you really like to do?"

"What I'm tempted to do, is just tell them Fred and I are living together. If they don't like it, they can lump it."

"But, obviously, you're not comfortable with that either."

"No, I love my parents. I don't want to do anything that would alienate them. I think Mother would understand, and she could live with it. But Dad is a strict moralist, and I don't think he could handle it."

It is always easier to set limits on intrusion by strangers, or on those with whom we aren't close. By far the most difficult people to fence out of our territories are our intimates. Because they are important to us, we often avoid having confrontations with them for fear it might change our relationship for the worse, or even alienate them.

Katy said, "I've never been able to stand up to my father. From the time I was a small child, he was always the boss. Mother always went along with what he said, even when she disagreed with him.

"I can't forget the one time I defied him. I was 16. He didn't want me to wear any makeup. I did it anyway, but only after I got to school or was with my friends. Then one day, my lipstick fell out of my purse. We had quite a scene."

She bit her lower lip to keep it from quivering. Some abortive tears filled her eyes.

"He spanked me."

With that, she wept openly, still fighting to hold back a flood.

"That must have been humiliating for you."

When she was able to stop crying, her expression changed.

"I've never forgiven him for that. When I went away to college, I rebelled with a passion. I not only smoked, I drank with my friends and slept around. Then I got frightened by my own behavior and settled down a bit.

"I was still rebellious when I married Jeff. He was a ne'er-do-well on campus, good looking, but trouble. Our little marriage only lasted two months. There wasn't anything in it for either of us; it was just another lark of two rebellious teenagers. My folks never found out about it. His parents had our marriage annulled. We were both relieved.

"The last two years of school were more of the same, but not as wild. When I graduated, Daryl and I married. After that, I became a middle-class housewife. Our marriage lasted four years. He was an adventurer, and left me for another woman.

"Dad was very disappointed in me but, since it was Daryl who left me, he couldn't hold me responsible, so he didn't say much."

"And now you're facing another potential crisis with him. What do you think he might do?"

"I don't know. I haven't lived at home in eleven years. I don't know if he's changed or how much."

"What's the worst that could happen?"

"He could disown me," she said, smiling. "But maybe I'll disown him first. No, I don't really know what he will do."

"It sounds as if you've almost made up your mind to play it straight."

"Yes, I guess it's time for both of us to face the reality that I'm a grownup with the right to chart my own course through life. He has a right to his opinions, and so do I."

Katy was struggling with the problem of limitations, how much she would permit her father to intrude into, and make policies for, her life. Where would she establish a "fence" that would allow him no further trespassing?

In her next interview following her parents' departure, she said, "Well, we all survived it."

"What happened?"

"I decided to face the issues directly. When we picked up Mom and Dad at the airport, I introduced Fred as the man I'm living with. Mother was so neat. She took it all in stride and she and Fred had immediate rapport."

"And your dad?"

"You could see he was shocked. He lapsed into a cool attitude, which lasted for the four days they were here.

"Before they left, Dad and I had a talk. He said, 'Now, I don't want to tell you how to live, but I must tell you that I disapprove of your living with Fred without being married. Your mother and I have had a hard time accepting the idea that you two are sleeping together.' I knew *he* had a hard time with it, but I don't think Mom did."

"What did you say to him?"

"I told him, 'Dad, I understand and appreciate your telling me. I know you want the best for me. But I'm a grown woman now, and the world is more different now than it's ever been. I have to make my own decisions about my life. I know some of my decisions will be mistakes, but I've made some and learned a lot from them. I respect your values and your point of view. I hope you can respect mine.'

"He shrugged his shoulders in resignation and said, 'Well, it's your life,' but I knew he wanted things to be different."

"How do you feel about the way you handled it?"

"I feel great. I don't know how Dad will deal with it, but I've resolved some important issues. *It was important for me to deal directly with him as adult to adult, and tell him essentially that I am the boss of me, and I will decide what is reasonable and appropriate for me to do with my life.*

"I think it was not only important for him to hear, but important for me to experience. I faced him as a peer, not as a little child asking for his approval."

I saw her again, a year later.

As she sat down in my office, she said, "Well, I'm back."

"What brings you to see me now?"

"I have my annual checkup with my gynecologist and my dentist, so why not with my psychologist?"

A review of the past year revealed continuing positive changes. She and Fred had married, and her relationship with her parents improved in many areas.

She told me, "You'd never believe it, but dad has become mellow in his old age. He is respecting my right to live my own life and make my own decisions — with my help, of course. I've had to slap his hands a couple of times when he got a little ambitious about giving me advice. But, all in all, things are going well."

As is the case with many people, when they change their relationship with their parents from child to parent, to one of two adults, they get along much better — if there were any relationship worthy of the name before. In order to reach such parity, the individual will have to go through a process of setting limits on how much intrusion he or she will allow on private territory.

Chapter **14.**

Mother Goose, Father Goose

*M*ost of us marry under the spell of the love myth. We are two lovers on a course to certain bliss and the solution of all our problems. What we all realize later is that, like Romeo and Juliet, we have brought two disparate clans and their complexities together. A frequent problem growing families encounter, but one seen most obviously in blended families, is the division into one team against another as the next interactions illustrate.

The two resentful people in my office were eager to have their viewpoints heard, as though they were dealing with an arbitrator. Each partner had a teenage son from a previous marriage and were struggling with the formidable problems the new blending presented. Both of them started to talk at once, stopped, started again, and then stopped, in an "Alphonse-Gaston" routine.

John, a 43-year-old real estate salesman, said in a half-joking, half-sarcastic way, "After you, my dear."

Lila, an office manager, just 40, said, "We're halfway to a divorce and want to know if there's anything we can do before we end this marriage."

"Why do you feel you need to end it?"

"We're at each other's throat much of the time. The good times have come and gone, and all that seems left is another fight. We were very much in love when we married ten months ago, but in the last four months, all we have left is the fighting."

"Give me a few examples."

Lila spoke quickly, "John's son, Robbie, is 16. He's rude and unmanageable and . . ."

John hurried to inject his comment, "Unmanageable and rude, sometimes, but you tend to be awfully particular and picky with him."

Before Lila could be sidetracked by John's comment, I said, "You were about to give me an example."

"Yes. Well, when we're all sitting down ready to eat dinner, Robbie will pick at his food and make insulting remarks about it. Then he'll let out a loud burp. John just ignores him. I say something to him and we're in battle. John makes all kinds of excuses for him and tells me I'm being too critical — in front of Robbie."

"How about another example?"

John spoke. "I'll give you one. Last night, Lila's son, Joel, was using foul language and abusing his mother. I won't tolerate that kind of behavior in my house."

"*Our* home," Lila corrected.

"O.K., *our* home. She shouldn't let that little punk talk that way to her. He needs to be taught a lesson. But when I tried to help out, Mother Goose here came out of the water and bit me."

Unable to contain herself, Lila said, "Joel didn't mean anything hurtful; he was only expressing his anger because I wouldn't let him use my car. John jumped right into it and threatened to wash Joel's mouth out with soap. Joel is a big, strong young man and he isn't about to take that kind of threat from anyone. He snapped at John, saying, 'Yeah? You and who else?' I had a terrible time keeping the two of them from tearing the house apart.

"I've been a mother as long as John's been a father, and I can take care of myself. I don't want anyone to butt into my relationship with my son."

"See? She excuses everything he does. No wonder he's such a brat."

"It does sound like Mother Goose and Father Goose protecting their little goslings," I said.

"What do you mean?" John asked.

"Well, it's apparent that both of you are fairly understanding of the behavior of your own son, but you can't seem to accept the same kinds of behavior in the child of the other parent. And if either of you dares to correct the child of the other, your parental instincts take over."

"But what am I to do when John wants to beat my son up?"

"I'm not saying it's wrong to be protective of your own son. That's quite natural. I'm merely pointing out that both of you are responsible for your part of the conflict, and that both of you will have to do something different in order to solve the problems.

"Both of you seem to be behaving like parents to the other's child."

"What's wrong with that?" John challenged.

"*Neither of you has yet earned the right to function as a* parent *to the other's son. In your new family, and in the eyes of either young man, you are not his parent.*"

"You mean, I have no rights as a parent?"

"Very little as yet, with Joel, but you certainly have rights in your role as a grownup in the family. That's very different from being a parent. Whatever relationship you two will have with the other's son remains to be seen. That will have to be worked out on a one-to-one basis."

"Are you saying I have to keep my mouth shut when Joel mouths off like a street kid?"

"You don't *have to*, but it would probably be better for your relationship with Lila, in the long run."

"Well, I don't see what's wrong with stopping Joel from abusing someone else."

"But Lila feels she doesn't need your protection and considers your action as an invasion of her territory when you do."

"Yes, I do. I have been dealing with Joel all his life and I think I've done a pretty good job. I'm a competent mother and don't need instruction in how I should behave."

"But do you see how you both intrude into the relationship of the other? *When it comes to conflict in the family, things work out better if two people can work it out one-on-*

one. If others get involved, it only gets more complicated and more difficult."

By thinking about their conflicts in the terms John suggested, the "Mother Goose and Father Goose" analogy, they were able to work out some of their problems. Understanding, of course, is only a first step. After that comes trial and learning. With practice, both people began to be able to stay out of the interaction of any other two people in the family.

Lila said, "I really had to bite my tongue a few times to keep from getting involved in Joel's and John's struggles, but I did it. There were times I got in my car and went for a drive. When I got back the house was still in one piece and both Joel and John seemed to have settled their issues without bloodshed."

John added, "I'll have to admit I slipped a few times and said more than I should have, but Lila was forgiving, and I've continued to learn. I almost jumped in when Lila and Robbie were going at it one day but, instead, I went out and mowed the lawn so I couldn't hear anything. When I came back in, they were baking a cake together."

Fortunately, Robbie and Joel got along well. In spite of a two year difference in their ages, Robbie liked and admired Joel, so that most of the work to be done was focused on the two adults.

This kind of "teaming up" of family team against family team is frequent and a source of much unnecessary difficulty for blended families. But the problems that occur in blended families through remarriage differs from those in first marriages only in the intensity of the conflicts. "Mother Goose and Father Goose" patterns occur there, too.

In a later interview, John expressed his feelings of impotence with Joel. "I sometimes feel unimportant in the family, especially where Joel is concerned. I like him and would like to have more of a relationship with him."

Lila felt the same way about Robbie. Both adults liked children and, naturally, wanted a stronger role in their new family.

"Since we've been working with the 'Goose' problems, things are much better at home, but I would like to play more of a part in Robbie's life. I've been tiptoeing around trying to avoid interfering with their business so much, I feel left out. There are times when I would like to take a parental role with Robbie. I don't mean I want to replace his mother. I just want to be more active in his growth and development."

"That's something we both want," John echoed. "We've made a lot of progress, and I think we can do it without the problems we had before. I want to be able to correct Joel as well as Robbie, and to guide them both. The problem is, I don't feel I have any clout with Joel. He goes to his mother for things he needs, and Robbie deals mostly with me. There must be some way we can be more involved."

"Are there some special interests you share with Joel?"

"You mean, like tennis or fishing?"

"Yes, something like that."

Lila suggested, "Joel is interested in mechanical things, like his bike. And you're good with the car. Maybe you could teach him some things about car maintenance. He'll be driving soon."

"Yes, and Robbie would like you to teach him to use your computer. Of course, he might only play games with it, but he'd probably go for that."

Lila and John each arranged to spend some special time with each of the young men. Although it is difficult for an adult to develop a close relationship with a teenager in a short period of time, they made good headway — for a while.

In a later interview, Lila laughed as she said, "We were going headlong into spending time with the two boys, and then found they didn't have time for us. They're both active young men and have a lot of friends. So we were feeling like the 'undated ones' sitting at home while our partners were out with someone else. So John and I started dating again, and we're finding we like it."

"Yes," I agreed. "You seem to have cleared up most of the pressing problems. Sounds as though you're through with me."

"Yes, I guess we are. But we'd like to know that we can come back if necessary."

"Well, I would like to see you. But let's hope it won't be necessary."

It was difficult to picture this contented couple as the resentful two I had seen only a few months earlier. *Freed of what they had earlier seen as the necessity to protect their child from abuse by an outsider, they were now freer to resume their interrupted love bond. Not only did they extricate themselves from progressively worsening conflicts, they freed up a great deal of time and energy for each other.*

These problems were worked out quickly because of the healthy base the two adults brought into the new family. They were both well functioning individuals and their sons were, too. Many problems of this kind don't have such a desirable ending.

In most situations, children are quick to seize upon a difference between the adults, to foster more dissension and conflict. In this way they can manipulate the situation to their own advantage. "Divide and conquer" is not a tactic only military forces can use. Such reactions are also natural attempts to maintain the integrity of their former family ties and to resist the new and unpredictable. Parents who do not recognize such maneuvers can get caught up in them and find their marriage disintegrating.

In another blended family, Emily was a very perceptive and understanding mother of two young sons and a teenage daughter who worked hard at testing the viability of their new blended family. One evening at dinner, she said in the presence of her new husband and her children, "Tanya said she doesn't like pork, and you seem to cook a lot of it." Tanya looked stricken as though she had been caught with her hand in someone else's pocket.

Emily's husband, Ralph, said, without looking up, "I'm glad Tanya feels free to express her opinions. I'll keep her preferences in mind when I cook, but I probably won't go overboard to please any one person in the family."

This interaction has some powerful elements in it that can teach us a lot. Emily's open sharing of a subtle criticism Tanya had expressed privately to her mother let Tanya know that anything she said about Ralph could be shared with him by her mother, so that no secret wedges could be driven between the two adults.

The way the two adults talked about Tanya, in her presence, placed her and the two boys in the role of eavesdroppers. Children will listen much more carefully to messages conveyed in this manner than in a direct lecture or instruction. Of course, that tactic has to be used skillfully to be effective.

Because Ralph was an outsider, in the process of winning a role in the new family, he needed "leverage." The three children, naturally, directed most of their conversation, questions and requests to their mother. When it was appropriate, that is, when it affected Ralph, Emily asked for his opinions, his participation or for his permission. Emily and Ralph went further in empowering him as a significant adult in the new family. Ralph began to have a major voice in vital areas when he became the buyer of groceries, and when he assumed the role of the allowance-giver. Emily retreated from the role of family chauffeur, and told her children If they needed a ride, they would have to ask Ralph. Ralph had been a skilled parent to his own now-grown-up children, so was able to use his powers effectively.

Emily was secure enough in herself and in her relationship with her children that she could share herself and her children with her new husband — two of the most precious territories she had. To make it work, Ralph fully appreciated the offers and dealt with them as the precious gifts they were. What was a blended family has, in the course of a few years, become a well balanced, integrated and extended family which also has kept reasonable ties with the children's biological father and his parents.

The successes of these two blended families contrasts with many other clans who have been much less successful. Their achievements have been limited to the extent to which the parents were able to share their vital territories of power and decision-making in relation to their children, as well as sharing themselves and their children.

Part 3.

Problems With Partners

Some problems that are "always there," have to do with our relationships with our partners, our lovers, our spouses, or associates of other kinds. The mere existence of such relationships guarantees problems between us. Understanding of the territorial aspects can help us to reduce such frictions or get rid of them.

Chapter 15.

Two Shall Become as One?

Two droplets of mercury tend to remain as two separate things. But, if forced together, they merge into a larger single droplet. Many of us are like that. We start out as separate beings but, in the course of living together, often function as an inseparable couple, at least in our own minds. Many difficulties we have with our partners stem from that psychological fusion.

Any system composed of two entities, including a couple, once united tends to remain intact. If something disturbs it, dynamic forces tend to make it return to what it was. But a couple is also naturally at odds with itself, as it is composed of two separate people. One of the most frequent problems they have is to determine which of the two people will be dominant over the unity.

When Sarah asked Erich, "What are we going to do today?" it sounded like an ordinary question — one that is asked a lot by people in couples situations. But the question implied that Sarah was asking the "boss" what the couple would do today, or implying that she was giving him the control over the "couple." If Erich weren't alert, he would get into trouble quickly.

However, Sarah isn't really being that generous because, if Erich had said, "We're going to watch football games all day," she would have quickly let him know she had some power over what the couple would be doing.

Sarah was apparently offering Erich something she really wasn't going to give. Actually, Erich sensed that, because he answered, "Uh, I don't know. What do *you* want to do?" His response was much more accurate than he realized. He truly didn't know what the couple would be doing. And he appropriately asked her what she wanted to do, instead of blindly trying to take control over the two of them.

Many of the battles between people in a close relationship occur in situations like these, when the individuals are unclear that there are three significant territories involved: yours, mine and ours. For example, one person might try to take control of the couple and make decisions for it, whether it is offered or not.

Erich usually returned home from work at the same time Sarah did. One night, he announced as he came in the door, "We've got to hurry. My boss is coming over for dinner tonight."

Sarah's immediate reaction was pure shock. For a moment, she was speechless. "Erich! What do you mean, your 'boss is coming over for dinner?' Are you crazy? I can't get a dinner together in an hour and a half. You call him and tell him it's all a mistake. I went on a trip. I'm in the hospital. Tell him anything, but he can't come to dinner on a moment's notice."

"You can do it. I know you can. His wife had to leave town suddenly to take care of her sick mother. He was feeling bad. It was my chance to get in good with him. He didn't have any plans, so I invited him to dinner."

Erich was at his persuasive best, and finally convinced Sarah to put together a dinner. Sarah heated a pre-cooked ham, opened a can of corn, whipped together a salad and baked a ready-mix cake. It wasn't her greatest creation, but Erich and his boss said it was a great meal.

After his boss left, Sarah said, "Erich, sit down. You and I are going to have a talk."

Erich, with his winning charm and beaming smile, sat down. "You were great. I knew you could do it. He was

pleased as punch."

"You're not going to be. That's the last time you ever pull one like that on me."

"Pull what?"

His feigned innocence didn't divert Sarah.

"If you ever invite someone over without consulting with me and getting my agreement, I'll fix you good. I'll pretend all is well, and just before your guest or guests arrive, I'll leave and go downtown and have dinner by myself in a fancy restaurant. Then maybe I'll take in a movie. You'll have some tall explaining to do."

"You wouldn't."

"Try me."

Her look and tone of voice were convincing.

Another kind of couples' problem occurs when one person doesn't realize he or she is intruding into the partner's domain, or attempting to acquire a partner's possession.

For example, Sarah complained about difficulties she had on the phone with a customer.

Erich, asked, "Why don't you tell that so-and-so to get lost? Who does he think he is? You should tell him he's a big jerk to talk to you that way. You can't let him get away with that. What you need to do is 'cut him off at the pass' — 'accidentally' cut the connection."

"But I can't do that. I'm the Customer Representative. My job is to correct those kinds of problems."

"Sure you can. You're going to have to take a firmer hand, if you want to be a success at the job."

"What makes you think I'm a failure at the job?"

"Well, obviously you can't handle a simple problem like that."

It doesn't take much imagination to picture what happened after that.

Sarah did give Erich an opening when she complained to him about the difficulty she had. Erich was quick to take over the problem and propose solutions, even though he hadn't been clearly invited to do that. In this case, the territory was a problem belonging to Sarah. Erich was unaware he was taking over by proposing solutions, and he didn't realize it even while they were describing the problem in my office.

And Sarah didn't see why she got so angry, other than that Erich seemed to be insulting her ability.

As we reviewed what had happened, Sarah saw that her complaint could easily be seen as asking for help, that is, inviting Erich into her territory. "I knew what I was going to do about it. I was just venting my spleen. I only wanted Erich to share my feelings, not take over the problem and treat me like a nincompoop."

"Then perhaps you need to make your message clear. Can you put it in terms that only ask for what you want?"

She pondered for a moment. "I guess I could say, 'I got upset today and I'd like you to just let me vent my spleen a little. I know what I'll do about it. I just need a sympathetic ear.' "

"That's a clear message."

I asked, "How might you handle it next time, Erich?"

Erich, at that point, realized he had tried to take over Sarah's problem. "Well, knowing that there are land mines lying around, I'll be a lot more careful about what I do when Sarah complains about a problem."

"So what would you do?"

"The first thing I would do depends a lot on how Sarah comes across."

"Tell us what you mean."

"Well, if she only complains about a problem, I guess I'll first ask her why she's telling me. If it's only to share information, I'll just listen.

"And beyond that, I guess I could ask her if she wanted my input before I gave it."

Discussing the problem in the framework of territories helped them to see some very basic reasons why they had conflict, and aided them in seeing some different ways to handle a problem that they might easily encounter again, with the same or different persons.

So if, as Erich, we aren't aware we are taking over someone's territory, we will be surprised when they become angry or aggressive with us. But we also need to be aware that we, as Sarah, sometimes behave in ways that seem to someone else an invitation to take over our possession. If that isn't what we want, we need to make sure we are sending clear messages.

These situations are aggravated by some of our cultural pressures. For centuries, many generations have been told that in marriage, "two shall become as one." Unfortunately, many people interpret that literally and try to function as a single entity. And when they do, it becomes a question of which of them rules.

Most of us were taught to be responsible. The problem is, we weren't helped to discriminate when we should and when we shouldn't take on accountability. So it is, when people see a problem lying there waiting for a solution, many of us jump in and take over the role of problem solver, whether the person owning the problem wants help or not.

Couples also get themselves into unnecessary complications because of another kind of territoriality. *Many love songs and love notes say things like, "Be Mine," "I'm Yours," "You Belong to Me," or "I Belong to You." And, after they belong to each other for a while, they start having fights to get some separation so they can regain clarity and possession of who they are. Neither of them wants to be a possession of the other, yet both promote such attitudes by the ways they interact.*

Also, for a long time, we have been led to believe that a couple of people who spend most of their time together makes for solid bonding that will last for a lifetime. In actual fact, *too much togetherness* shortens *the life of the bond. Depriving ourselves of the alone time, which all of us require, violates a natural rhythm of needs, and places an unnatural and increased stress on the relationship.*

In one interview, Sarah said, "We enjoy a lot of things together, but there are times I just want to be left alone. Erich wants to be close to me all the time, and put his arms around me and kiss me. That was great in the beginning, but it's now beginning to bug me.

"He wants to go everywhere I go. There isn't a time when I can be by myself to read, relax or even take a nap."

"Have you told him you need some alone time?"

"No, I don't want to hurt his feelings."

"Are you saying that it is better that you hurt your

own feelings than say something to Erich and risk hurting his?"

"Am I doing that again? It's so hard to take care of myself, sometimes. But if I don't tell him, how can I expect him to know?"

The next week, in an interview with both of them, Sarah was able to deal with the problem. She told Erich, "I want you to hear me out, and not jump to a lot of conclusions. I need some time to be alone, away from everybody, including you. It's not you. It's me. I need time by myself to recuperate, to rest and be by myself. I want to be able to tell you when I need that time, without you feeling hurt and guilty."

Erich looked hurt. "Why now? You've never needed to be alone before."

"No, that's not true. I've *needed* to be alone from time to time all my life; I just haven't loved myself enough to provide it. I'm now asking you to be considerate of my need to have some solitude. You need to be alone sometimes, too. You withdraw into yourself sometimes when you go fishing, or when you go hiking or sometimes when you crawl into the TV 'tube.'"

"Well, yeah. I can leave you time for yourself, if you really need it."

"I *really* need it."

"O.K., you've got it. Just let me know when."

That wasn't the end of that problem. They still had to work at it so they could eventually arrive at agreement on when and how the alone time would be taken and given.

Togetherness and being alone are opposite ends of one aspect of a relationship. For best results, we need to have a rhythm of alternation from one to the other. If we have too much alone time, we get lonely. If we have too much togetherness, we get restless, bored, or start a fight. Achieving a balance of the two — which changes with each situation — requires sensitive awareness of our own needs and the other person's needs, as well as an appreciation of the reality situation in which we find ourselves.

Rather than seeing ourselves as part of a unit, a couple, we need to recognize more clearly that we function best as two separate people in a relationship.

Chapter **16.**

When Parents Disagree

*A*ll parents disagree, and sometimes about the most basic things. Arguments between them about how to deal with their children are the most common and frequently disturbing events in families. There are some real and constructive solutions, but only a few parents ever find them. The frictions usually have their cause in the intrusions of one or both into the other parent's territory. The solutions require that each parent be clear about his and her own domain of responsibility, and that each stay out of the affairs of the other.

Martina and George, parents of two teenage children, entered my office and sat on opposites ends of a couch, without looking at each other. It didn't take much sophistication to guess how their relationship was going.

Martina, a woman in her early forties, spoke first. She said, "I think we need help. Nothing is working well. George and I can't get along, and the children are unhappy."

I asked, "What is happening?"

"George never supports me with the children. Whenever I scold them or discipline them, in any way, he interferes."

That aroused George, who had been content, up until that moment, to remain in the background and listen. He said, "That's a lie. I don't interfere. I don't say a word, even when she's outrageous."

"No, you don't *say* anything, but your actions scream your attitudes. You smirk, you slam your paper down and you stomp out of the room. The children aren't stupid. They know how you feel."

Martina and George had plowed this ground over and over, with little result beyond their growing resentments toward each other. The battles were over which of them was right, which way was best and sometimes they fought over who would dominate the other.

Their two children, Nora, who was almost 12, and Carey, who had just become 16, were much affected by the constant bickering and the inconsistency of the different viewpoints of their parents.

Nora's school performance had deteriorated and she had developed many nervous habits. She would break into tears for no apparent reason. Other times, she withdrew into her bedroom and hid from the rest of the family.

Carey reacted quite differently. He allied himself with his father, who seemed easier and more lenient. Toward his mother, he often showed a contemptuous attitude. When she refused him some privilege, he turned to his father — who usually went along with his wishes. Naturally, his manipulations intensified the friction between Martina and George.

Nora and her mother were very close. Martina protected her in every way. When she and Carey argued, Martina always sided with Nora. She defended her actions by saying, "Carey's a boy, and much bigger. He could and would hurt her if I didn't stop him."

What Martina didn't know was that Nora, in her little quiet way, was able to defeat Carey over and over. By her seemingly "weak" behavior and weeping, she easily won her mother's alliance. None of the other family members realized what was going on. Another thing the adults didn't see clearly was the two "teams" set up in the family: Father and Carey vs. Mother and Nora.

Martina and George were decent and concerned parents, but viewed their roles as parents quite differently.

Martina said, "I believe it is our responsibility as parents to teach our children to respect the law and become responsible citizens." She tried to teach them to live by the Golden Rule. Knowing that children would slack off, if given a chance, she guided them diligently and followed them closely.

George wanted the children to have an easier life than he had when he struggled through his own childhood. He recalled with pain, "My father was killed in an accident when I was twelve, so I had to go to work to help my mother provide for the five of us in the family."

His mother had treated him much as Martina dealt with Carey. He looked back on his mother's heavy-handedness with resentment and reacted to Martina's treatment of Carey in the same way. He said, "I don't want my children to have the same kind of childhood I had. In my opinion, Martina pushes Carey too hard."

Both Martina and George thought they were preparing their children for life as responsible, happy adults, but they each saw the other as going about it in the wrong way. In this respect, they were like most parents.

They both assumed there was only one "right way" to bring up children and that they were in possession of that method. After all, those ideas were based on their life experiences and logic. The problem is, the same thing is true for each of us, but we've each had different lives. Those different experiences naturally lead to different conclusions, and none of us realize how different until we run into problems.

Early in their parenting, George and Martina agreed they should present a united point of view for their offspring. They arrived at what they thought were mutual decisions in dealing with their children. What they didn't realize was that their concepts of what they were agreeing to were quite different.

Had they realized how different they were, in their views and ideas, and had they appreciated each other's reasons for them, they might have been able to come to realistic agreements and understandings. But, as so many of us, they naively assumed everyone felt, thought and acted from the same foundations.

*George and Martina are like many people who be-
come a couple. They lose sight of themselves and each
other as individuals, and begin to think of and deal with
each other as part of the same unity. And, as part of one
thing, there should be no disharmony. Although as a spiri-
tual idea, "two shall become as one," can be helpful; when
it is taken in a literal way, it creates enormous difficulty and
misunderstanding.*

George and Martina learned in the process of counseling how very different their approaches were. They also began to see that *a parent has a right to have his or her own
kind of relationship with each child in the family, without interference by others. That relationship is a territory "owned"
by the child and the parent.* They agreed that the only time
it might be necessary for interference by a third party
would be when something serious or dangerous was occur-
ring. Both parents admitted they didn't think the other was
doing anything seriously damaging to the children.

It was difficult for each to allow the other parent to deal
with the children in their own ways, but they worked diligently at it. What they discovered was that both approaches worked, to some degree.

These parents were only vaguely aware that they were
contesting for control of the decision-making territory in the
family. During one of the many arguments between them in
my office, I asked, "Which one of you is the boss?"

The argument stopped. They looked at each other.

Martina spoke. "I think we both are bosses."

"At the same time?"

They both smiled in embarrassment.

Martina asked, "Do you think that's why we are having
so many problems?"

"What do you think about that?"

My question was an evasion, but it was intended to get
George and Martina to deal with the problem, and struggle
to find an answer which would be their own, instead of
hearing someone else's ideas about it.

Martina said, "Yes, I think that's part of the problem."

George added, "I would agree. Sometimes it's a question of which one of us is going to be the Big Boss."

In the course of that interview, they realized they were both responsible for interfering with each other's parenting. They also saw, clearly, how destructive it had been for the family.

Martina said, "I have been guilty of interfering with what George was doing, and trying to get him to do it my way. It's so hard to let things be."

"I've interfered with Martina's discipline, too. I guess I was trying to be the Supreme Leader."

Gradually, they were able to see and accept that a parent had a right and a responsibility to have his or her own kind of relationship with each of their children. Neither of them should interfere with that.

That led to their acceptance that any contention between any two people in the family was best kept on a one-to-one basis. They agreed to try to keep those ideas in mind as they worked with the problems.

Martina later reported one way she had handled a problem at home, "I was explaining to Nora how I wanted her to set the table. George was watching and listening, but I could tell he was determined not to say or do anything. Carey chimed in with some advice. I told him that Nora and I were dealing with the problem. If he wanted to get into a discussion, he'd have to arrange one for himself at a later time. Right then, I wanted him to get out of the dining room. He *re*sisted, but I *in*sisted. And George stayed completely out of it. I appreciated that."

George had a similar encounter with Nora, and Martina didn't interfere, he reported.

In family conflicts, "Two's company; three's a crowd." Any two members of the family who have difficulty with one another — after the youngest is about four or five years old — if left to their own devices, will resolve their issues. The ways they find acceptable might not be acceptable to others, but they usually work.

Many years ago, in the days of black and white movies, I remember seeing one about the French Foreign Legion. In the story, a dark-skinned man told about the reasons for having more than one wife in his culture.

"If you have one wife, she may be lonely. If you have

two wives, they are company to each other — but they may fight. If you have three wives, two will always get together against a third. But if you have four wives, they will each have company and, if they fight, it will be two against two."

Without getting into the question of polygamy, those observations about the effects of the number of people in an interaction have much in common with our observations about people in our culture. As indicated above, two individuals can usually find a solution to their problems. If three people are involved, two will team up on a third. And the two against two situation was true in George and Martina's family.

Incidentally, when a committee is formed to arrive at recommendations, three members would appear to be an ideal number to arrive at a majority decision.

George and Martina worked diligently to stay out of one another's business in the family. As a result, their conflicts with each other diminished greatly. They began to enjoy each other once more, and a unity of purpose in relation to their children emerged.

Martina described an incident that illustrated the change in her relationship with George:

"One night at the dinner table, George said, 'Carey told me you were a very crabby mother, and he wished he could have someone like Paul's mother.' Carey looked stricken. I said to George, 'Well, that's too bad. He's stuck with a crabby mother.'

"The way George handled that was beautiful. It told Carey that he would no longer be able to drive a wedge between George and me, and it let Nora know, also, that we were a parent team working together — not against them but *for* them."

Nora's behavior also changed. She was less and less the shrinking violet. She dropped the "sickly child" appearance, and looked and acted like a normal child. She and Carey began to have ordinary arguments, as other brothers and sisters do, but they also did more things together and for each other.

Carey became more active at school. He joined a soccer team and spent less time with his father. Because his mother wouldn't tolerate it, and because his father no longer supported his rebelliousness against his mother, his contemptuous attitudes disappeared.

Family outings, which once had been minor disasters, began to be more fun.

But that phase of family life didn't last long, as both children were teenagers and beginning to spend more time with their friends.

George and Martina began to get reacquainted after their alienation of a few years' standing. They joined a couples bowling league.

Clarifications of the territories in the family led to fewer violations, to fewer battles and to better relations between them.

No two families will have the same problems, but the "divide and conquer" tactic can be found everywhere. Is it causing you to lose perspective?

Chapter **17.**

Be
Reasonable

Imagine two people sitting side by side in a rowboat, each wielding an oar. One wants to go forward; the other wants to reverse. As each paddles, the boat goes in a circle. Their plight is similar to that of many couples who can't agree on which way to go.

Marcy confronted her husband with "obvious facts." "You know Art is being unreasonable with Madge. You just take his side because he's your friend, and he's male."

"Now that's a dumb thing to say. Be reasonable, for heaven's sake. It's plain as oatmeal. Madge is being ridiculous and you know it. Art is an expert in his field, so he should know. Just because you don't know anything about it, and she's your friend, you take her part."

Alvin and Marcy were having another of their frequent arguments, edging into name calling and resentment. The situation is ordinary and frequent in the lives of many couples, so their interaction has much to teach us.

Each of them is trying to persuade the other to "Be reasonable. Think the way I do." And each of them is resisting the persuasions of the other. For either of them, to agree with the other seems like capitulation.

Yet most of us have observed that outsiders can persuade

one or the other partner of a couple to consider a particular viewpoint when neither of them will listen to their partner.

At a party, Barney, a neighbor said, "An expert always has to be from out of town, or people tend to disregard what he says."

Alvin seemed impressed. "That's true. I never thought of that."

Marcy appeared offended. "I told you that last month when we were at mother's."

Alvin looked at her in puzzlement. "I don't remember you saying anything like that."

Marcy turned on her heel and joined some other people in the next room.

This interaction is an excellent illustration of the verbalized insight the neighbor presented: Alvin couldn't accept Marcy as an expert, as she was too much a part of his intimate life, i.e., she wasn't "from out of town." He promptly dismissed what she'd said as not especially profound or important, and forgot it. But Barney is not a part of his very intimate circle, is therefore "from out of town," so he was one who had an "expert's" insight.

The same reactions are seen in groups. Alvin's local professional group planned to have an expert speak to their organization. Ed, a member of the planning committee, suggested, "Why don't we ask Bill Wilson? He knows a lot about the subject we're interested in, and he's an entertaining speaker."

Another member of the committee objected, "We can hear Bill Wilson anytime. What I'd like is an expert from the outside who can give us some really new information."

Ed persisted, "But Bill's a very creative person who always has a new wrinkle in his thinking."

He was quickly and thoroughly outvoted.

Alvin said, "It's really strange. Bill Wilson is respected by everyone I know. But when it comes to having a speaker for the group, they won't for a minute consider him. It has something to do with him being local. He may know a lot more than somebody from another place, but the one from the outside is an "expert," and Bill's not. It's just as our neighbor, Barney, said, 'An expert has to be from out of town.'"

All of us have participated in these kinds of interactions, or at least have witnessed them. *One reason we can accept a stranger's ideas more easily than those of someone close to us is that, in a close relationship, we are subject to a million obvious or subtle influences from each other all the time we are together. If all of those influences were to be accepted and became part of our personal territory, our ownership and control over it would become ambiguous.*

An analogy might make it more clear. If we permitted a neighbor to move his furniture into our home, it would soon become less and less familiar — and less and less our own. At some point, we would be forced to stop the influx or lose our territory.

That is what often happens to couples. Because each of us is exposed to so much continuous influence from our partners, we have to fend off some of it from time to time. The rejection of input occurs when we have had too much of it, rather than because it is bad, wrong or illogical. This kind of vulnerability arises when two people exercise too much influence over one another, and when they lack clarity about who they are.

The fact that any two people who spend much time together become powerful influences on each other can be easily accepted. But many of us wouldn't recognize some of the signs of that power.

For example, Alvin complained in one interview, "Marcy has such a negative streak in her. If I have an idea or a suggestion, or if I express an opinion, nine times out of ten, she'll disagree with me."

It would be very difficult to convince Alvin that he has great influence over Marcy. He equates influence with agreement and compliance. But if she weren't so much influenced by him, she could agree, disagree, or ignore what he said. But to disagree so much, so often, with his points of view is itself evidence that she has to fight off his influence so she won't succumb to it.

The argument they had at home about their friends is also a resistance to being inundated by a partner. Each of them is trying to get the other to agree with his and her point of view. In essence, they are saying, "Be reasonable.

Be like me." *Both of them resist, for the same reason: to maintain their identity boundaries, and remain who they are, unchanged by the other's efforts. Their reactions are understandable as self defense.*

However, unless both people understand what is taking place, they will put a different meaning on the interaction. For example, they might see each other as "stubborn and pigheaded," or as always having to be right, or always trying to dominate. Then it might justify being angry and righteous. Each conflict then becomes damaging to the relationship, very much as each bite in a tree the beaver takes weakens the structure, so that eventually the living structure collapses.

But if a person understands the defensive reaction, and can recognize his or her own role in the frictions, it is then possible to manage it differently. *A person needs to respect the right of others to be who they are, without trying to mold them into a duplicate of oneself. And we need to respect the right of others to have and to express their opinions even if they are different from our own. As long as they don't intrude into another's domain, they have a right to be and act as they do.*

Couples who have been together for a long time, often lose sight of themselves and their partner as separate individuals, and react as if they are a single entity, a couple. That creates a problem. Any disagreement is seen as an attack on the one "in charge." If both people assume they are in charge, there will be a power struggle to see which of them shall be dominant.

For example, Marcy said, "I think I have a right to be offended when Alvin says and does stupid things. It's a reflection on me."

She is taking the position that Alvin is hurting the couple in some way when he says or does something "stupid." If she and he are a single entity, that may be true. But clearly, they are two people in a relationship with each other. She may not like his behavior, but it doesn't hurt her or violate her rights in any way.

If she were totally responsible for Alvin, she would be right. But since they are both adults and separate individuals, Alvin is responsible for his own behavior. And if she chooses to feel embarrassed by his behavior, that is her choice, and she still has no legitimate complaint against Alvin.

However, if Alvin shares with others in a group one of Marcy's indiscretions, he *is* hurting her, and she is justified in feeling betrayed and angry. He has violated her right-to-privacy territory.

On another occasion, Marcy was most uncomfortable with Alvin's driving. She asked, "Would you mind driving a bit more carefully?"

"Stop telling me how to drive. *I'm* driving."

"I'm not telling you how to drive. I'm asking you to be considerate of my life and limb. You're risking my life as well as yours."

"If you don't like my driving, why don't you get out and walk?"

"I think that's a good idea. Let me out."

Marcy took a cab home and from that time on, drove her own car. In this instance, what Alvin was doing did affect Marcy, did endanger her. She was justified in asking him to do something different. Instead of tolerating his attitude and participating in risking her well-being, she did the sensible thing and removed her self territory from the situation. She was disagreeing with him — and being reasonable at the same time.

Mind Your Own Business!

Chapter *18.*

Breaking the Shackles

*B*oth men and women have viewed the possession and use of anger and aggression as the province of males. It is only in recent times that some women are able to express such emotions, but acting *on anger and* being aggressive *is still generally forbidden for women. It's now all right for women to be assertive, but not aggressive. The latter is commonly regarded as the same as being "hostile" — but not for a man. Such a one-sided view is as handicapping, to the female of a male-female couple, as having one arm tied behind the back while trying to fight.*

Donna, a business manager of 28, complained of anxiety attacks which interfered with her work.

"I don't know why they're happening. Everything seems to be going along quite well. I just got a favorable evaluation from my supervisor. And everything at work is going along swimmingly. I just can't understand it."

"What else is happening in your life?"

"Nothing special. My dad just retired and he and my mom are driving around the country in their camper-bus. Jerold and I have been living together for nine months and that's going well."

"When did the anxiety start?"

"Last week."

"What kind of a week was it?"

"About the only thing I can think of that was significant was an argument that Jerold and I had."

"Tell me about it."

"He'd been using my car because he sold his. He's been dropping me off at work and picking me up at night. Last Saturday, I had to work for a few hours. When I got up, Jerold was gone, and so was my car. I had to take a cab to get to work and back.

"I didn't mind his taking my car, if only he'd told me he would be using it. He knew I was working that day. Anyway, I told him he should have asked to use my car, or make arrangements so we could both be where we needed to be.

"He was mad. He called me a few choice names, so I asked for my car keys. He threw them on the floor and stormed out. He said I was a hostile, selfish bitch."

"What made him so angry? Was there more to the argument than you've described?"

"Not much. But that's the first time I ever expressed dissatisfaction about anything to him. I guess he was shocked by it. I'm sorry I got on him. I guess I was being bitchy."

"Do you mean *you* were out of line in being angry?"

"I guess I could have been nicer about it."

" *You* could have been nicer about it?"

From this exchange, it was apparent that Donna was buying into a lot of cultural stereotypes: that an angry woman is a bitchy woman, that, in conflict with a man, she's usually wrong, and she should be "nice," no matter what. In the retelling of the events, she totally ignored Jerold's aggressive and thoughtless behavior in taking her car, his abusive language to her and his lack of responsibility in placing all the blame on her. She was almost ready to assume all the blame for being bitchy, and "forgetting the whole thing."

Aggression and anger are only two of their many tools women must learn to use to deal with problems of male-female equality. Advising women to discard them is like telling a carpenter to throw away her hammer because it won't saw wood. Tools are of value when they fit the need and are used with skill. The moral: collect as many tools as you

114

need and learn to use them as well as your talents will allow. Take self assertiveness courses. Take the aggressive ones: Judo and Karate. And don't be afraid to use what you learn.

Cultivating our own self territories by discovering our many potentials and gifts, and learning how to use them effectively are parts of growing up and blossoming into the most we can be. We will focus more on self development in Part IV.

Donna gradually came to accept that being angry and acting in an aggressive way was relevant and appropriate under some circumstances. She learned to assert herself more in a variety of situations.

In one interview, she said, "I now know what you meant when you said that being aggressive in protecting myself was a loving thing to do for myself. I had to do it yesterday, and it's having a powerful impact on me.

"It was late afternoon, and I was opening the door to my car when someone yanked on my purse. It has a strong strap, and I had a good grip on it. I grabbed it back from a teenage boy, and kicked him where it hurts. He ran and I chased him until he disappeared around a corner. It's the first time I ever did anything like that, and I started laughing and couldn't stop. Since then, I've had a sense of exhilaration and well being."

Donna's self esteem continued to improve as she stood up for herself and as she became more assertive. She had discovered that her anger and aggression, which she had so carefully and guiltily stored away, were valuable inner resources that she could, on occasion, use in productive and creative ways.

In spite of the progress made in the direction of equality of the sexes, there is still a long way to go. In many ways, women are their own enemies. But the ways aren't always recognized for what they are. Many otherwise modern women still promote their own shackling without realizing it. They have been their own "keepers" in the sense of "jailers," when they could be their own "keepers" in the sense of being caretakers of their own domains. For example, when Tina and her accountant husband, Fred, decided to buy a home, Tina favored a Colonial one, but Fred preferred a Contemporary. She yielded to his choice — and yielded and yielded. Five years later, she was in my office with anxiety attacks.

"I should have known better," she said. "First, it was the house, then the furniture. He chose the way the yard was to be planted, the kind of cars we bought and the ways we invested money. I felt myself and my desires being crowded into a tiny corner.

"Fred made me account for my time each day and would ask why I didn't have a half hour to squeeze in a trip to the lumberyard. I probably could have, so I began to feel guilty about that."

Without their clear realization, she and Fred were recreating the age-old male dominance pattern. Fred would ask the questions, Tina would answer them. Fred could use his aggressiveness and self assertion; Tina was to forego her own. By not being fully aware of her own aggressive endowment and cultivating skill in using it, she was permitting herself to be pushed aside and dominated.

"You don't seem to be aware that you work hand in glove with Fred to keep you in chains."

"I don't know what you mean."

"You were saying that Fred wants an accounting from you each day, and you comply by giving it to him."

"But how is that helping him to control me?"

"The one who asks the questions sets the direction and leads the way; the one who answers the questions follows."

"I'm still not sure what you mean, but I'll think about it."

In another interview, Tina was describing a conversation with Fred about her mother's forthcoming birthday. She asked, "Do you think it would be all right to buy Mom a television for her birthday?"

Fred's response was that they were in a tight money situation and she should look for something less expensive.

As she described the predicament, she was obviously frustrated.

"Our money situation isn't that tight. We could easily afford it. But I didn't want to make an issue of it, so I gave in."

I asked, "Did you need permission to buy her a gift?"

"Well, sorta. Fred takes care of the finances."

"What do you mean, 'takes care of the finances?'"

"He banks all of his money and the money I bring in, pays the bills and makes the investments."

"Did I hear you say 'his money'?"

"Yes. I mean the money he brings home."

"And what do you call the money you bring home?"

"That's our money, too."

"Wait a minute. I'm not sure I understand. The money he brings home is 'his money,' and the money you bring home is 'our money'?"

"Of course, it's all *our* money."

Her readiness to drop the matter here characterized her avoidance of many difficult issues. By avoiding them, she avoided unpleasantness, but was then saddled with an increasing number of handicaps in the relationship. Her passivity and reluctance to engage in confrontive interchange with Fred allowed him to take control of the power territory and dominate.

"I'm hearing two very different messages from you: On the one hand, you feel backed into a corner because Fred runs so many things; and on the other hand, you don't mind giving up your power."

"Could you explain that a bit more? I'm not sure I understand what you mean."

"You don't seem to like it that Fred chose the home, planned the landscaping, picked out the cars you bought and made all the investments, and yet you keep giving up the territory of decision making."

"How do I give Fred power?"

"You said that Fred wants you to account for your time, and you dutifully report to him. And then you give him the power to manage the money. Then the money he brings home is 'his money,' while the money you bring in belongs to both of you. But more than that, you apparently don't even protest or argue the points with him. It's as though you're not allowed to be outspoken or confrontive. If you don't participate in making decisions, you're giving up the power to decide."

"The reason he manages the money is that he's so

much better at it than I am. I can't even balance the checkbook."

As many women do, Tina was playing dumb about being able to manage money and balance the checkbook. She was assuming there was some kind of magic to it, and she didn't have it. Under pressure, she admitted she could learn to do it. She admitted that it only takes effort — and possibly a good calculator.

Women who give up the territory of participating in all their financial matters are setting themselves up for subservience. Money in this society represents power, and the one who manages it is the one with the most power in the relationship. Each person needs to be aggressive enough to assert equality.

In another interview, Tina was complaining about having so much to do.

"Sometimes I wish Fred would help more with the chores."

"How do you mean?"

"Well, we both work, so we don't have too much time except on weekends. Taking care of the house, cooking, doing the laundry and shopping for the groceries takes so much of my time."

"What part of the homework does Fred do?"

"He sees that the cars are kept in good running order, and does some of the yard work that the neighbor boy can't do."

"Are you saying that you feel you have more to do than Fred does?"

"Yes. I know I do. After work, I have several hours of work each evening before I can go to bed."

"Does Fred agree with you that you do more of the domestic work than he does?"

"I think so. I asked him if he didn't think it would be fairer if he helped me to get some of the things done. He agreed, but he forgets and then I have to remind him. Sometimes, I have to show him how it needs to be done. Last week, he snapped at me, 'If you want me to help you, you're going to have to quit nagging.'"

"You asked him to 'help' you?"

"Yes."

"If he 'helps' you, who owns the domestic job?"

With some difficulty, she began to realize how deadly that word could be. She saw that she had assumed ownership of much of the domestic work, as her mother had.

"But after all this time, what could I do about it? It would be impossible to get Fred to change things now."

"Impossible?"

"Well, it wouldn't be easy."

"Do you want to go on in the ways you have been? Or do you want to change things?"

"I want to change things. I want a better break."

"Then you might have to fight for your rights."

"Fight?"

"Yes. You might have to stand up for your rights and try to get Fred to make some changes."

The next meetings were devoted to preparing her for such talks with Fred. After that, she and Fred dealt with the issues and Fred agreed to make some changes. Tina was surprised that it was much less difficult than she had feared. She found herself able to say some difficult things and to assert herself enough to ask him to make some changes. She was using her own aggressive energies to take care of herself better.

Tina learned about another deadly word. Because she spent much of every day taking care of their six-year-old daughter, she said, "I asked Fred if he would baby-sit Danette so I could go skiing with some women from the office. He was good enough to do it a couple of times, but later, he complained, 'I'm getting tired of doing your job. After all, you're the mother.'"

"You used the word, 'baby-sit'?"

"Yes."

"Do parents '*baby-sit*'?"

She blushed as the implications hit her.

"How many more ways do I sabotage myself?"

Once more, Tina had to have a problem-solving talk. Fortunately for Tina, Fred was willing to examine his own attitudes and behavior, and to change some of them. *It's not always that two people can work out their problems in such* a satisfactory way. But a woman who finds a man unwilling to try, will have to make the hard choice of remaining a serf or breaking the shackles, whether by dissension, aggression or divorce.

Chapter **19**.

Climbing Out of a Rut

*O*ld shoes are often more comfortable than new ones until the new are broken in. It's human to try to keep things the same, even though we feel limited by our ruts. Expanding horizons in life is interesting, but can occasionally be frightening and uncomfortable. The conflict between comfort of the old and the challenges of the new sometimes creates problems between partners.

When Rick and Joyce entered my office, the tension lines in their faces and their serious demeanor announced their disturbance. They were hardly seated when Joyce blurted out, "I don't see why Rick always has to change things. Why can't he be happy with what he has?"

Rick responded, "Joyce seems to take change so personally. She sees any change I want to make as an attempt to leave her behind. It's not that. I just want to try something new."

The situation in my office was beginning to sound like a court of law, with two sides presenting cases to a judge. But as it is always important to hear them out so that I can understand their viewpoints, I let them go on to see why they were having difficulty.

I didn't understand the source of their conflict, but it appeared Joyce felt more vulnerable. First, I had to establish some understanding of her position.

"Joyce, it sounds as if Rick's changes have a heavy impact on you."

"They do. I feel out of step with him, as if I'm running to catch up with him. And when I do, he takes another turn and I'm left wondering where he went."

"Joyce, that's not . . ."

"Whoa, let her finish, Rick." I gestured like a policeman directing traffic. They reminded me of impatient drivers at a busy intersection, each hesitating only briefly before charging ahead. But, if Rick didn't pause a little longer, a collision was likely.

"Continue," I said, with a nod toward Joyce.

She glanced at Rick, as if to be sure he would let her speak freely. "Just after Rick and I met, he began jogging — that was something new for him. I'd drive him to his 10-K runs and root for him, you know, pinning his race numbers on his singlet, looking after his warm-up suit, packing him a lunch, and all of that. I had never seen myself as athletic and, gradually, with his encouragement, I also began to run. To my surprise, I liked it and discovered that I was really pretty competitive. I could hold my own."

"She did better than hold her own. She won a lot of ribbons."

His statement wasn't condescending, but an affirmation of his pride in her accomplishments. I nodded to acknowledge his statement, and Joyce continued.

"About the time I got comfortable with the idea of being a successful runner, he switched activities."

Rick moved forward in his chair, as if ready to charge into the conversation, but once again, I flashed a stop sign. He slid back while Joyce elaborated.

"Almost overnight, he quit running and started swimming and then competing at Master's swim meets."

"And how did that affect you?" I asked.

"I felt abandoned. I had enjoyed our training together, talking about magazine articles on running and planning for upcoming races."

"So you felt a certain intimacy in the shared activity. Was that lost when he started swimming?"

"Yes, and when I tried to tell him about my feelings he would get angry with me."

After getting a chance to express her point of view, she was ready to hear Rick's reply. All he needed was the green light to begin.

"Rick?"

"We ran a lot and it was great fun. I think running meant something a little different for me than for her. I liked the competition with other men and also with myself. When I trained, I usually had specific goals in mind, a certain pace I wanted to maintain or a personal record I was shooting for."

"How do you think your reasons were different from Joyce's?"

"The winning didn't seem as important to her. I think the closeness that came from sharing an activity with me was more important to her."

Joyce nodded in agreement.

"What drew you away from running?"

"The change wasn't as sudden as Joyce may have thought. Actually, it took me about a year to make the switch. After a while running became repetitious. It was too predictable, too routine, for me. I still wanted a competitive outlet that would keep me in good shape but running was becoming a rut. About that time, I developed a stress fracture from overtraining and my physician suggested that I find a non-impact sport while I was recovering."

"Why didn't you tell me that?" Joyce asked.

"I didn't think it was all that important. I didn't want to lose the cardio-pulmonary benefits I had acquired from all my training. If I just sat around and waited for my leg to heal, I would have been losing ground. So the sports medicine doctor said that an activity that didn't involve running or jumping, an activity like bicycling or swimming, would keep me fit without aggravating my injury."

"And that's when you dove into the pool?"

"Yes, and I found the newness stimulating, the freshness of the new setting, techniques, and competitors exciting."

"Were you aware of the impact your change in sports was having on Joyce?"

"Yes, I couldn't help but recognize how she felt," he said with a warm laugh, apparently his way of turning down the heat of their tensions.

Joyce smiled in self-acknowledgment and said, "I do tend to be rather outspoken. I don't hide my feelings very well. When he began swimming, he did it with such enthusiasm that I became jealous. It was as though he'd found a mistress."

"In what way?" I asked.

"He seemed more excited about his new sport than he did when we ran together. He started speaking with the new terminology, talking about techniques I knew nothing about. It was threatening."

"I tried to reassure her, to tell her that she was the beneficiary of my new enthusiasm. The challenge made me feel more masculine, more self-confident and it even carried over into our lovemaking."

"Did you feel only a sense of loss, Joyce, or did you also benefit?"

"It's true. He was very attentive and affectionate."

"So your switch to swimming wasn't an attempt to keep your wife at arm's length?"

"No, not at all. I love being with her and sharing activities. Maybe that's why we fought so much. I wanted to try something new but I also felt guilty spending time away from her."

"That doesn't make any sense to me, Rick. It sounds like you want to have your cake and eat it too."

"Sometimes we appear to act in opposition to the way we feel," I said. *"The reason we fight so hard sometimes is to oppose our own inclination, our desire to yield to the other person."*

"That doesn't make any sense," she said.

"Rick said that he felt guilty about taking up a new sport. There was a part of him that probably felt it was betraying you, but there was also another part that wanted to explore the unknown. By arguing with you, he was able to act out that internal struggle. When you opposed him you represented that part of himself that didn't want to change. The harder you tried to resist his change, the more power you gave to his opposing tendency."

"That sounds like a lot of gobbledygook," she said with a smile. "I'm afraid that's 'way over my head."

"Maybe an example will help, one that is familiar," I said. "Rick's torn feelings, wanting to comply with your needs and his wish for something new, is a dilemma we witness in most teenagers.

"When a teenage girl begins dating, and settles on a steady boyfriend, her parents often become apprehensive about her emerging sexuality. Sometimes very subtly, but just as often directly, they begin pressuring her to find a new boyfriend because they know that the physical temptations will be there for the young couple. The temptations are there and, on one hand, she'd like to be more active sexually, because of the pleasant physical sensations and emotional closeness it brings. But she is also fearful for the same reasons her parents are fearful. She might fear pregnancy, violating her religious or personal values, losing her reputation, any of a number of valid reasons."

"So she would feel the same as I did," said Rick " — desiring to take the next step but also not wanting to."

"Yes, but if all she hears from her parents is 'No, No,' then their persistent negative pronouncements tend to drown out the girl's own inner voice, which is also saying no. She doesn't even hear her own opposition because it's overshadowed so strongly by the voice of her parents."

"So, the only voice she hears is the other one within her, the one saying, 'Yes,'" Rick said.

"And she acts on that one," said Joyce. "I remember my first boyfriend was a boy my parents didn't like. He was actually a little scary for me because he was so different, so unpredictable. His rebelliousness frightened me. But the more they said I shouldn't date him, the more I wanted to be with him."

"*Their opposition only gave more strength to your curiosity about the unknown.*"

"But if I didn't protest, Rick would be off trying everything new."

"Honey, I don't have the time or energy it would take to jump continuously from one new activity to another. To become a successful swimmer requires the same investment of years of effort required to become a competitive runner. It was hard for me to give up running."

"You sure never showed it." She lapsed into thoughtfulness. "I still wish you were a runner, not a swimmer."

I spoke to Joyce, "The shared intimacy was important and you are experiencing a feeling of loss because of it. But it's important to realize he's not rejecting you."

"I guess I have a hard time being sympathetic with his need for a change. I only feel deserted."

"Think about your favorite book for a moment. How often have you re-read it in the last year?"

"I haven't read it in a year or two. I've probably read it only twice."

"Why so infrequently?"

"I see what you're getting at. It wouldn't hold my interest enough to re-read it now. I'd rather read a new novel."

"And that's how it was with my running," said Rick. "It had become too routine. I wanted a new challenge even though the old one had been very special for me. I felt I'd exhausted that arena. I was ready for a change."

"But what about your loss of intimacy, when he stopped running?"

"I guess we really haven't lost it. We're still close in many ways, even if we no longer run together. I thought, since we were married, we should do everything together, and when Rick wanted to do something different, it was as if he were leaving me. I can see now he was off on another book, another chapter."

That was the beginning of Joyce and Rick's being able to accept each other as two different personalities who could grow in different directions without breaking up.

Some months later, they returned for a progress evaluation. Joyce looked happier and less worried..

"We've been doing 'our own thing' for some time, now, and I'm finding new freedom in pursuing activities Rick doesn't share. I've gone back to school to study History and Philosophy, and I'm finding some deeply satisfying experiences in learning."

"Yeah, she's turning into a real professorial type," Rick said.

"We've found that our interests overlap only a little, and that we each have some that the other doesn't share. In spite of that, we aren't losing interest in each other. We're each finding the other to be more interesting because we're bringing something new and different into our old relationship.

"I'm embarrassed to admit that I, too, felt cramped by my tendency to keep everything the same and my reluctance to try anything new. Now, I'm discovering a lot of interesting things about myself and about Rick. I've stopped thinking of myself as a dull drudge, and even find some entertainment in discovering what I can do quite well. Every day seems like opening a new book to read and understand."

Both Joyce and Rick were finding the joy and refreshment that comes from expansion and use of their self territories. The more they discovered about their own and each other's talents, interests and capacities, the more they liked and valued.

When we stop growing, we start to die. That is true of all living creatures. The "dying" is often similar to what happens in a pond which has no outlet and the springs which feed it dry up for the summer. The water stagnates and becomes unfit for use. Renewal begins with new freshets which introduce nutrients.

All living creatures need new influx of stimulants to bloom. Joyce and Rick were rediscovering that, even though they had experienced it many times before, and would rediscover it many times ahead. Providing those nutrients for the expansion of our beings is our own basic "business."

Chapter **20.**

Differences That Attract — And Repel

*T*he difference between a man and a woman often sparks their interest in each other. But those same differences can also cause discord in their lives.

After introductions in the waiting room, I invited the well groomed, serious couple to my office. Julie walked quickly down the hall, while Deryk ambled after her. Inside, Julie chose a seat on the sofa and sat down; Deryk seated himself next to her, but not close enough to touch.

In response to a question, Julie responded immediately, "Deryk and I are having a lot of conflict. We've tried to solve the problems on our own, but decided we need some outside help on this one. Don't you agree, Deryk?"

Deryk nodded, silently.

Julie continued, "I'll give you my viewpoint, and then Deryk can give his. I think Deryk is thoughtless and inconsiderate of my feelings at times. And talking with him, if he isn't in the mood to speak, is little better than chatting with the Great Sphinx. It's maddening. Sometimes I wonder if I even exist for him. There are times when I think I could drop dead and he would just pick me up and lay me on the bed and call the undertaker. I have to initiate everything — even our lovemaking. It makes me feel the way I did in Junior High, with my long skinny legs, freckles and funny face — an absolute nothing. He never compliments me, no matter how hard I try to please him."

Throughout this spirited outburst, Deryk sat impassively, apparently listening, but not seeming to be angry or even perturbed.

"How do you see it, Deryk?"

After some pondering, he spoke. "I guess she's right."

Julie leaped out of her seat. "You guess I'm right? Don't you have anything else to say? Why don't you tell the doctor that I nag, I swear, I scream at you? Why don't you tell him I'm always picking on you and criticizing you?"

Deryk said quietly, "Yes, you do, and yes, you are."

Julie sat down hard, crossing her arms and legs. "You see what I mean? He gets angry but he won't talk to me. He just emotionally walks out and sulks alone."

When Deryk began to speak again, Julie seemed surprised. He said, "I don't say much because it gets me in trouble. I have a lot I could say and have wanted to say, but Julie thinks faster and talks faster than I do, so I never get to finish what I have in mind. I also don't like to say things in anger because I'll regret it later, so I like to think before I speak."

"But at least I'd know how you feel. We could discuss things and find some kind of solution, instead of living with this silent frustration."

I kept my gaze on Deryk, signaling that he still had the floor.

Deliberately, in measured tones, he said, "I used to talk a lot more, but I found I got overruled and it led into nothing but arguments, so I decided to keep my mouth shut."

"You two have very different 'fight styles.'"

"What do you mean?" Julie asked.

"When you get into difficulty with Deryk, you want to lay all your cards on the table, discuss it in the here and now and settle things."

She nodded, waiting for more.

"And you, Deryk, like to 'go up on the mountain' and think about it, until you come to some conclusions. Then you're ready to come down and talk about it."

"But he never comes back and talks."

"Would you be willing to give Deryk some time to think about it before you two discuss it?"

"But he never comes back!"

"Would you be willing to give him some time to think?"

"Yes, if he'll talk to me in a day or so."

"Deryk?"

"Sure."

"Could you also tell Julie when you need to think things over, and about when you'd be ready to talk?"

"I can do that."

That was only the beginning. With preliminary agreement, we had to "walk through" several arguments before they developed a pattern that did lead to resolutions — instead of revolutions.

This contrast in the ways they approached conflict resolution was only one of many very significant differences between these two people. Many individuals, some professionals included, think any *difference can be eliminated through counseling. Some can. Others can be mediated, as this one was. And some discrepancies stubbornly remain in spite of much therapy. In partnerships, where there are a great many sharp contrasts, few will survive "'til death do them part," because our lifetimes are about twice as long as they were in Biblical days. Also because the mere existence of dissimilarities creates tension, which can slowly fracture partnerships.*

All of us can live with tension — for a while. But over time, stress tends to accumulate, and many differences create tensions faster. For every instance of lack of compatibility, making adjustments leaves tension — every time the two people are together. *Two or three* major *adjustments are ordinary, but ten or more create continuing, extensive stresses in the individuals and on the relationship, as they did in this pair.*

The difference between Julie and Deryk, of how they dealt with problems, is one that can be modified, but it can't be eliminated. Where the difficulty has to do with mis-understanding — or with not understanding — the issues can be removed, sometimes permanently. But *when the disparities arise out of the makeup of our personalities, they are very durable.*

In the next few weeks, several frictions that were due to misunderstanding, and those that were due to lack of un-derstanding were resolved. Julie and Deryk were getting along much better.

In the next interview, Julie complained, "Why can't you be neater and better organized?"

"I probably could, but it wouldn't be worth it to me."

"It would be worth it to *me,* and we'd get along a lot better."

"Deryk, why wouldn't it be worth it to you?"

"If I took the time to neatly fold my dirty laundry, turn the socks inside out, and sort them into the 'right' piles, squeegee the shower stall, always put the toilet seat down, wipe out the sink after I used it, and make my bed with the corners neatly made — every single time — I'd either have to get up a half hour earlier or be late for work. I don't think all those things are reasonable. If Julie were employed, that might be different"

"But there's a right and a wrong way to do things."

"Yes, the right way is your way, and the wrong way is anybody else's."

"That's not fair. I don't claim to be always right."

"You don't *claim* to be, but you make the message clear in other ways."

Julie said, "I like my way of doing things, but Deryk has his own way, and I don't like a lot of his ways."

"You two have a lot of differences, and many of them aren't going to be changed in the future. If you're to live together, you'll need to make accommodations to each other, to 'live around' the ones that aren't going to be erased, and allow your partner to be the way he or she is in those areas."

In the ideal world, each person would change a little and then live happily ever after. But fairy tales are for enter-tainment and solace, not blueprints for living.

Julie said, "I'm a morning person. I like to get a head start on the day. But 'sleepy head' here, likes to sleep in, so I have to twiddle my thumbs until he decides to wake up."

"Why do you have to 'twiddle your thumbs'?"

"Well, until he gets up, I can't do much without making noise."

"Isn't that boring for you?"

"Yes, but I guess I just have to 'live around' that obstacle."

"You mean that you couldn't find something interesting to do that wouldn't depend on his being there?"

"I guess I could."

The next week, Julie arranged to play tennis early in the morning with some old friends she hadn't seen for a while. She had found a way to 'live around' one problem of their diversity.

Julie and Deryk resolved many other minor issues in the weeks we worked together, but now, they were facing the more difficult and the durable dissimilarities.

For example, Julie tended to do everything fast, where Deryk tended to be more easy going and unhurried. This was one of the differences between them, which attracted them to each other originally, and which now was a source of tension.

This tempo difference was basic to their personality makeup, and could only be modified. Every time they were together, Julie had to remember to slow down, and Deryk had to remind himself to speed up. Each time they made the adjustment, it left a residue of tension.

When they went to social get-togethers they always argued, so that they arrived in tension, and left for home in another argument. Julie said, "Our friends invite us for dinner, and the least we can do is be on time, but Deryk drags around and we're always late. As a consequence, I'm disgruntled and don't have as good a time."

"Yes, that's true. By the time we arrive, I'm not in much of a party mood. Julie wants to be there right on the dot. I know our friends don't expect everyone to show up that promptly. I don't like to be pushed to be on time when it doesn't matter. And just about the time I get un-tensed and am beginning to enjoy myself, Julie wants to go home."

I asked, "Must you go to these engagements to-gether?"

Julie responded, "Well, what's the use of being married if we do everything separately? Besides, it's more expensive to run two cars than one."

"But what about the cost to you both in terms of tension and resentment?"

They resolved this issue by driving separately. Julie arrived promptly and left when she felt it was time. Deryk enjoyed his more leisurely pace. The first time she arrived at a party alone, however, Julie had to explain why they were arriving separately.

Julie was well organized and felt most comfortable when everything in her environment was neat. Deryk was more casual, but not a slob. He always knew where to find his things, even though Julie considered him disorganized. Their long established routines were subject to little change. Julie consciously made an effort not to nag at Deryk to "neaten things up," and Deryk exerted effort to be some-what neater in areas that they shared.

In another interview, Julie complained, "I can't ever have my friends over."

"Ever?" Deryk challenged.

"Well, hardly ever. You either refuse to be there, or you offer to stay in your den while the party's going on. I won't have anyone over on those conditions."

"That's up to you. I don't see why I have to be the good host or the good guest every time you get an invitation. If you like them, you go. I'll go to some, but not all — and sometimes I'll participate in entertaining at home."

Their bitterest quarrels came when they decided to buy a house. Their tastes, of course, were different. Julie wanted a Colonial; Deryk preferred a rustic dwelling. Julie wanted to live in the suburbs; Deryk preferred a rural setting. They agreed on a Colonial on the edge of the city, which pleased neither of them. The choice of furniture triggered the biggest arguments. Deryk wanted some very casual furniture in the den. Julie wanted traditional throughout the home.

Of all the couples with whom I have worked, these two

people had the greatest number of disparate preferences. In all they did, they seemed to go in different directions. Both people made heroic efforts to accommodate the differences, or to avoid confrontations about them but, no matter what they did, they inevitably stumbled on another problem. For over a year, they struggled to work out their problems and find a way to live comfortably together.

In our last interview, both people seemed serious, but less tense, even sad. Julie spoke first, "We've decided to hang it up. We both know we've given it our best shot, and still we're a long way from being happy or even satisfied. Before we get back into hating each other and behaving like street urchins, we thought we'd better quit while we're ahead. We wanted you to know we appreciate what you did."

Deryk said, *"We've come to realize that neither of us was trying to hurt the other. We were only being who we are. You can't blame a cat and a dog for not getting along. It's in their natures. They're too different for comfort, and so are we. I like Julie and would like to be her friend, but I know if we keep on living together, I won't be."*

Many times along the way during the time we worked together, I wondered to myself whether they could "work it out," and live with all their many differences. I wouldn't have been surprised at any time if they had given up. To their credit, they tried harder to try to save their marriage than any couple I had seen. The fact that they didn't have children made their parting less complicated, but the pain remained..

Perhaps many partnerships today find the going rockier than in the past, when long courtships and more active participation in their choices of partner by their parents gave them more opportunity to discover some problems before they married.

Julie and Deryk's decision was an extremely difficult decision, but one that seemed a sensible one to them. No one could accurately describe their decision as frivolous or lacking in effort.

Chapter **21.**

The Passionate Experience — It's Not For Everyone

A *unique occurrence, which a few people will experience, often goes by with little notice. It is similar to and, therefore, mistakenly regarded as the garden variety of "falling in love." Only some people are privileged — or doomed — to undergo it. It is an experience that is ten times more intense than ordinary love involvements of a man and a woman. It is important to territoriality, as it transforms the precious identity territory in very significant ways. It is best described as* The Passionate Experience.

Vanessa, a 29-year-old accountant, said, "I'm afraid I'm losing my mind. I can't sleep. I can't eat. I find myself doing things I've never done before. I love Allan so much I can't bear to have him out of my sight. If another woman so much as looks at him, I want to scratch her eyes out. I've never been a violent person and I've never been jealous. Am I going crazy?"

Of course she wasn't going crazy — at least not in the usual sense of the word. She had been married to a nice guy, named John, and they did all the ordinary things married people do. Then one day, John announced he was in love with another woman and wanted a divorce. It took Vanessa the better part of a year to recuperate. Then she met Allan, and fell hopelessly into a deep emotional abyss. She had been "in love" with John but that was nothing, compared to the all-consuming, blinding passion she felt for Allan.

"I was no innocent before I married," Vanessa said. "I've always enjoyed sex, and it was good with John, but I've never known the intense excitement, deep arousal and ecstasy that Allan and I have. I know the difference between having sex and making love, but this is another kind of experience entirely."

The interlude of harmony was short lived, as conflicts began to intrude. Vanessa complained, "When we fight, he leaves and stays away for two or three days. I'm just out of my mind until he comes back. My friends ask me why I put up with it. Since they haven't experienced this, they can't understand it. It's like an addiction."

Allan, 35, described his emotional situation in similar terms. He said, "God! I'm so crazy in love with Vanessa, I can't stand it. When things are going right, it's fantastic; but when things go wrong, it's the deepest part of Hell. She just can't let things be. She's always suspecting me of looking for another relationship, especially when we fight and I have to get out of there."

"Why do you 'have to get out of there'?"

"Because she comes at me with her claws, throws things at me — or, like last week, she came at me with her son's hockey stick. I was afraid that if she hit me, I'd punch her out."

Allan had divorced his first wife because both of them were bored with the marriage and each other. Allan said, "We never had an argument. It may sound a bit weird, but I couldn't stand the peacefulness of it. I used to wish she'd get mad at me, raise her voice or tell me to go to hell. Isn't that nutty?"

"So now, you have the fights?"

"My God, yes. But I didn't want this many of them."

In the middle of the experience, both Vanessa and Allan would gladly escape from the anguish if they could, but they knew they would, at the same time, be separated from the closest they would ever come to that sense of ecstasy. So they stayed.

Most of the people who undergo this experience are quite ordinary personalities before they embark on a radical emotional voyage from which they return transformed. It is like a fire in which their basic metal is converted from one kind of being to another with very different characteristics.

One of Vanessa's friends said, "I don't know what's happened to her. She's a completely different person from the Vanessa I knew. Before, I could almost predict what she would do under almost any circumstance. I could count on her to do whatever she said she would do. Of all the people I knew, I would have said she was the most emotionally stable."

"And now?"

"Now, she's emotionally unstable. One minute, she is quiet and calm; the next minute, she can burst into tears, have a temper outburst, be cutting and sarcastic, or apologetic. I'm not comfortable with her anymore. I don't know what to expect."

Vanessa described some of the inner changes that were reflected in her reactions outside. "I used to be a very controlled person. But that was on the surface. Other people might not have known it, but I've always been an emotional person. Since I met Allan, I do and think a lot of things I would never have done before. I feel my emotions more deeply than I ever thought I could.

"I never realized I could love someone as deeply as I care for Allan. I didn't know I was capable of the intense passions I've felt with him. And I'm troubled about the intensity of my other emotions and things I do.

"You mean the jealousy?"

"That, and my rages. I've never 'lost it' before, like I have with Allan. Once, when he bought a new car, and was so enamored of it that he seemed uninterested in me, I had a fit, and bashed in the windshield. He slapped me, and we had a physical fight on the street. The police came and separated us. We said some awful things to each other. I worry about myself."

Allan was feeling some of the same emotional intensity as Vanessa. He said, "I've always been considered by people who know me as a pretty steady guy. Now, they look at me as if I've changed into something they don't understand. When I talk to some people, they seem as if they were ready to run if I start acting crazy."

"You feel you sometimes act 'crazy'?"

"Well, maybe not the usual kind of crazy, but certainly different than I've ever behaved before. Really, I am different since I met Vanessa. No one has ever meant that much to me, not my mother, my father or any of my family, and we're a close family."

"And you also feel other emotions that strongly?"

"You mean anger and sadness? Definitely, yes. I have never been known to be a guy who gets 'down' and withdrawn, but I have times when I get that way. When Vanessa and I have an argument and break up 'forever,' I'm devastated until I hear from her again."

"Is that why you drop out of sight for two or three days?"

"Yes, I don't want to see anybody. I just want to slink off and 'lick my wounds.'"

Both Allan and Vanessa were discovering some new things about their inner territory of emotion. They were experiencing the greatest of fulfillments and the heights of happiness, but the price they were paying was in exquisite pain, terrible anxiety, irrational jealousy and tormenting conflict. Neither had known such intensity of emotion before, and had no idea they could be so deeply aroused. Had they known they were headed for such powerful emotions, and had they had a choice, they might not have chosen to undergo the experience. But of course, they didn't know, and had little choice.

What makes The Passionate Experience *so volatile is the unique mix of circumstances. In nature, it is like the excessive closeness of Mark and his mother in Chapter VIII. Lovers are too close, too long. That kind of closeness can be deeply fulfilling and satisfying — but it gets much more complicated. It is like bringing two critical masses of radioactive elements together: it leads to powerful repelling forces.*

Though Allan and Vanessa were unaware of it, they were not only strongly attracted to each other, they were powerfully driven to escape from each other. Our cultural bias, in favor of thinking we only have one emotion at a time, prevents us from recognizing that our emotional dispositions are usually ambivalent. The drive to escape arose out of the deep anxiety their excessive closeness stimulated. Each of them was only aware of attraction and need to be close. Neither of them would allow recognition of need to be away from the other.

Any close relationship, if continued too long at any one time, results in gradual loss of clarity of the boundary between the two people, leading to loss of clarity about what is "I" and what is "you," or loss of the most crucial territory of all: one's personal identity. In ordinary circumstances, most people manifest a rhythm of togetherness and separation that allows for renewal and confirmation of the self boundaries and preservation of the self territory. But the Passionate Experience *is not ordinary, and two people in that condition stay too long together and lose clarity of their selves. That arouses more and more anxiety until it forces separation. This is often described as fear of intimacy. Actually, everyone has, and naturally should have, some fear of intimacy, as it is potentially a major threat to our functioning integrity — if it is excessive — and* the Passionate Experience *is excessive in every way.*

Allan and Vanessa ignored their own inner needs to reaffirm their identity boundaries until the urgency erupted in fights. Fights are a most primitive and most effective means of achieving distance. Without their awareness, Allan's and Vanessa's unconscious needs for separation emerged in cooperative action. Like a couple of well trained dancers, they coordinated their efforts to produce a distance- and security-producing fight. Everyone in a close relationship participates in such distancing when it is needed. In the absence of better methods, these kinds of fights are constructive and necessary — even though they may also be troubling.

The sharp difference between Allan's first partner and his second is like Vanessa's. It is no accident that the *Pas-*

sionate Experience comes later; it takes a bit of psychological preparation. It is also not coincidental that the second partner is diametrically different from the first.

People who go through the experience are usually older than 30, and the passionate interlude is their second or third major intimate relationship. Most of them are very controlled people, conventional and predictable. They are persons who seldom lose their tempers or express strong feelings — until the change. After that, their emotions are free flowing, impulsive and loosely controlled for a while. Only much later are those emotions re-harnessed and brought under better control.

For a partner, they choose someone who is able to "trigger" the long contained emotions, helping them to be more freely expressive, emotional and active. *It is a neglected side of their personalities which is stimulated into development.* Before, they had, for the most part, "lived in their heads." And now, with the awakening of their emotions, they have to live life more completely, in their bodies as well. But learning to live with all these new feelings and emotions is difficult. This newness is partly responsible for the conflicts that occur, as emerging emotions are impulsively vented or clumsily expressed.

One of the more frequent traumas these individuals experience was described by Vanessa. She said, "Can you believe it? Something very personal and intimate that I shared with Allan, he told someone else when he was angry with me! I trusted him more than anyone I've known and he betrays me like this!"

Excessive sharing backfires. When we are plunged into this passion we tend to share too much. We put all twelve eggs in the basket and then have to worry about disaster. In any fight, people usually strike at the "Achilles Heel" of the other. So what would be more natural than to strike at the vulnerable and exposed tenderness of the psyche, the shared secrets?

Contrary to much of the nonsense we hear today about being totally "open," relationships are as much preserved and sustained by what is not shared, as by what is. Total sharing is juvenile and abuses the notion of honesty in relationships.

We all hear that not only should we be "totally honest" and "let it all hang out," but that conflict is good for the relationship. Constructive conflict *can be good, but the kinds of contention in which people engage most of the time lead neither to understanding nor resolution. This latter kind of friction chips away at our caring so that, eventually, the entire foundation is weakened and the relationship collapses.* This is precisely what happens to end some *Passionate Experiences.*

Although the participants are wholly unaware of it, they often contribute to the ending of the bond, cooperating to create a climax and an ending. It is as if both persons felt unable to continue in acute vulnerability so they cooperate to end it.

Increasing frequency of fights usually signals the ending of *The Passionate Experience.* In this oscillation stage, the lovers quarrel, separate in anger, only to return to the delights of making up — and then repeat the procedure. Not only do the frictions occur more frequently, they often take on more violent forms. The oscillation continues and intensifies until one or the other achieves "escape velocity" and they part for good. Allan and Vanessa were in the middle of oscillation.

Most of these relationships end within 6-18 months. The more fiercely and intensely the passions burn, the quicker they end. Only a few of these powerful experiences continue on and mature into a solid commitment. The ones that endure are those in which both people are mature and in which both have more than the usual capacity for persistence — or where external circumstances force the two apart on a regular basis so they can't engage in the excesses.

Although Vanessa and Allan didn't think so at the time, an enforced series of separations, which intervened in their beginning oscillation, turned out to be fortunate. Allan's father became seriously ill, which prevented him from continuing to run the family business 800 miles away. He asked Allan to take over until he could return. Allan was torn between his sense of obligation to his parents, and his own need to remain with Vanessa. He finally reached a compromise solution. Although it would be expensive, he would commute between his father's business and the city where he lived. He could spend weekends with Vanessa.

Vanessa, who was completing work for her graduate degree, couldn't move for a year. She said later, "I didn't know if I could manage without seeing Allan, but we managed quite well. I found I could devote more time to my studies, which I badly needed to do. I had been neglecting them to be with Allan. I feel guilty saying this, but there was relief in not being together so much. Besides being able to devote more time to my studies, I found I enjoyed being by myself at times. I needed it."

Progressively, over the next few weeks, Vanessa and Allan adjusted to the new circumstances and separations. Allan told her, "In some ways, this separation has some good points. Each time, I look forward to seeing you again even more. And have you noticed? We don't have as many fights."

"When Allan told me that, I realized it was true. Our relationship was too intense. Now that we've been forced to be apart, I can see the blessings of being apart on a regular basis. It wasn't what I wanted before, but I like it, now."

During the time they were apart, Vanessa discovered that, when they were together too much, Allan became restless and testy. She correctly identified the behavior as need to be away from her — to reconfirm his own identity boundaries. She took the initiative to arrange with Allan to take some time apart from each other, sometimes only an hour or so. He agreed, with some sense of relief, she thought.

A real test came when Allan got a ten day break. His brother took over the business during his own vacation. Allan and Vanessa planned a trip by auto along the Coast.

Vanessa said, "I've made an agreement with Allan that we will schedule some separation time every day. I'm surprised that he agreed to it, but he also recognizes that we need some time apart."

They returned from the ten days, refreshed and happy, because they had avoided even the little frictions. In time, they developed a healthy respect for the power of their emotions. *They recognized the necessity for separation time so that their boundaries could be reestablished, and cultivated skill in such necessary maintenance.* When Allan's father returned to work, He and Vanessa were able to resume their regular time together without the former intensity.

The Passionate Experience *they had isn't simply an aberration. Their success in surviving it isn't frequently seen. But even if it doesn't ripen into a long lasting relationship for most people, the residue and fallout are lasting. The effects turn out to be a little short of remarkable, comparing favorably with the best results of thoroughgoing psychotherapy. The individuals emerging from it are more complete persons in the sense that they have welded together the thinking part of their personalities with the emotional part in a more well rounded configuration. After that, they find they have a greatly expanded potential for richer and deeper relationships.*

The Passionate Experience is a golden opportunity, a double-edged sword of experience which cuts both ways. The pain of it can't be escaped. It is all one with the joys, a part of life's rhythms. The cost is high, but the product is durable and priceless.

Part 4.

The
Self Territory

In this fourth section we will focus on problems we all have with a very special type of territory that determines the kind of life we will live. This is our self, our Identity, our grasp of who we are, the most precious territory we shall ever have. As with other territories, we have to win it, define it, label and defend it, and spend the rest of our lives cultivating it. It is our compass that provides a sense of direction to what we do. As our home base, it is a haven to which we can return to replenish our energies. It provides a sense of security, familiarity and comfort. But, as any turf, we can lose it, neglect it, and have it stolen or abused. We need to cherish it, protect it and nurture it and, like a good friend, it will return the favor a thousandfold.

Without clear identity, we will feel an ever-present insecurity. We will encounter much difficulty in our relationships with other people and be limited in the degree of intimacy we can have with them. Poor self esteem and lack of self confidence will be our constant companions.

On the other hand, well cultivated identity will give us much greater control over our lives and how we will live. It will provide us with a greater capacity to enjoy close relationships with those we care about.

In this part, we will focus on problems we all have with the most important of territories, our self, our identity — who we are. As the most central, most precious and most interesting domain we shall ever own, much of our concern will be here.

Chapter **22.**

Someone to Watch over Me

Some of the first betrayals we suffer are the hardest to accept:
- learning that there is no Santa Claus;
- meeting with the first broken promise;
- discovering that our parents are only human;
- finding that law and justice are only approximate;
- and learning that the cherished relationship can end.

From these experiences, our innocent trust in "security" gives way to the relative and the probable.

One of the eeriest experiences we can have is to be in silent, pitch black darkness. Several years ago, during some sensory deprivation experiments in which the amount of stimulation to a person was reduced to a minimum, strange things happened. A blindfolded volunteer was placed in a rubberized suit and submerged in water to maximize the isolation from noise, smells, sights and gravity. After a few minutes the volunteer began to imagine he could see lights and hear sounds and noises. Then he began to experience hallucinations. Shortly thereafter, panic set in and the volunteer had to be brought to the surface and released from the experiment. From those studies, scientists realized that our sense of contact with our environment is dependent on our moment to moment stimulation by touch, sights, sounds and other sensations.

When we don't have that continuous yet changing stimulation, we start losing contact with reality.

Most of us spend much of our time and energy searching for something in which we can have unshakable trust. Without it, many individuals remain anxious and tentative. We look outward, in vain, to find something we can depend upon with certainty. For some, a religious or mystical faith becomes the one stability in their lives. For others, science is the faith that provides meaning and steadiness. Life for many people becomes a constant search for someone to care for them and allay their fears. For a few others, the discovery that they, themselves, can be counted on to the last is a source of comfort.

Al, a man in his eighties, told me in an interview, "The one thing I could always count on was me. After everybody was gone, I was still there. And if anybody was going to do something for me then, I was the one."

Another man, Gordon, who was 76, said with intense bitterness, "There's nobody you can depend on. They get what they want, and when you need 'em, they're gone."

The contrast between the views of these two old men highlights the importance of cultivating and clarifying our identities. Only when we know what we can and cannot do, and have tested ourselves over and over, can we have some measure of confidence about relying on ourselves.

Al was, in a true sense, his own best friend.

Gordon had no one — not even himself. He had failed to cultivate his own most precious resource.

Both these men had suffered much deprivation in their childhood. But Al was now secure and facing the end of his days with a serene resignation. Gordon was beset by deep anxiety and despair.

Al said, "My parents were killed in an accident when I was five. I lived with several different relatives until they had as much of me as they could stand and then I got moved again. Things were always changing for me. I couldn't rely on someone else to provide things for me — or even to be there very long."

He learned from that an invaluable lesson: he could provide for himself most of the "mothering" he needed. He could acknowledge his own excellence, recognize his own accomplishments, praise his own efforts, comfort himself, and take care of his physical and emotional needs. Beyond that, he could love and respect himself, avoid being cruel to himself, take appropriate responsibility without self blame, be sympathetic without being maudlin and show respect for others and for himself. Because he had a clear sense of who he was, he could accept others' opinions, criticisms or suggestions for what they were, and accept or reject them according to his own judgment. Clarity about his identity was the product of a lifetime of diligent work.

Al's struggle was much like the kinds of work we must do in all areas of our lives.

When we establish our first home, we acquire it, then make of it a nest of our very own. We plant our kind of bushes and flowers, build our kind of fences or walls, and decorate according to our preferences — however wild or tasteful. We outfit it with the necessities of furnishings and tools, and can then relax to do other things.

In like manner, we do the same in discovering who we are. We gradually become more clear about our talents, our values, our shortcomings, our personality characteristics and our aims. Just as animals gain a sense of security when they have won and defended their territories, we too need to win, hold and cultivate our most precious territory: our identity. Only when we have a reasonable command of it, can we more easily go about to do other things in life.

A clear sense of who we are is never won for all time. Nor is our idea of who we are completely accurate. Our self concept, as it is called, is only approximate. It is like a map of the entire territory. It is useful as a guide. The more accurate it is, the more helpful it can be, and the more reliance we can place on it.

Like the continuous tending of our plantings, the weeding, the fertilizing and watering, our identities are also dependent upon continuous reinforcement. It requires a constant attention to the differences between what is me and what is not me. That attention is learned and practiced; the discriminating is work and takes energy.

When we are with someone unclear about his or her

identity, we must work harder, as they tend to wander in and out of our identity boundaries.

Beyond learning to be clear about what is ours to deal with, the ease and efficiency with which we deal with life's problems depends on our clarity about ourselves: who we are, what we believe, what our abilities and capacities are, what we value or don't, what we will stand for and won't, what our aims are, etc. The more thoroughly we know ourselves, and value ourselves, the easier and less cluttered is our path through life and, we know where we can find the most reliable person to watch over us.

Chapter **23.**

Must We 'Clean Our Plate'?

*S*ome lessons we learned in our childhood continue to be entrenched in our lives, even though they may be outdated or have even become obstacles. Many customs and disciplines of our younger years need to be put away when we grow up; some old habits need to be jettisoned.

Ann, a graduate student at a local university, consulted me about such a problem. She said, "To do or not to do it? I'm enrolled in a Master of Business Administration program. I thought I wanted my MBA, but now after this first quarter, I don't think the program is for me."

"What makes you think so?"

"The pressure. I don't like the pressure."

"What pressure?"

"The pressure to do well in school, to grind out the papers, to keep up with the reading. It's just too much work."

"Do you feel other pressures, too?"

"Yes. The tuition expenses. I can't afford them. I don't like going into debt to finance the program."

"Those are financial costs," I said, suspecting there were some hidden expenses of other kinds. "Are there other personal costs?"

"I'm not sure what you mean."

"What impact is school having on your personal life?"

"I'm a single parent. I have two children and the MBA takes too much time away from them. I get too frantic, too rushed. Last quarter I was a mess, my kids were a mess and my job was a mess."

"That sounds very stressful."

"It was. And now, the second quarter starts in two weeks. I bought eighty dollars worth of textbooks on Monday for my upcoming classes, but after looking them over, I don't know if I should keep them. The classes look so dull. They don't appeal to me at all. But I made the decision, so I guess I'll have to live with it."

"You can't change your mind?"

"And quit? I'd be afraid to admit it to my family and friends. They've all been so supportive. No, once I start something, I've never quit. I was brought up to believe that I should always finish what I started."

"You should always 'clean your plate'?"

"Yes. I was taught that if I filled my plate with food, I had to eat everything I took."

Tears welled up in her eyes. "It's so hard to know what to do. I don't want more school right now. I'd rather be doing anything else, but I feel obligated to finish."

"For whom are you going to finish the MBA program?"

"For me, of course."

In her next interview, she continued to struggle with the problem. She said, "Last time, you asked for whom I was going to finish the MBA. I had answered that it was for me, but the more I thought about it, the more I realized I was doing it for everybody *but* me. *That's what I've been doing for most of my life. I've continued into my adulthood being the good child, and doing what my parents and grandparents wanted me to do. But then, I wondered if they really wanted that or if I merely thought they did.*

"In the past year, I've been having a terrible inner struggle, trying to decide what to do. My family members have all told me I was too impulsive, so I learned to be more deliberate, more considerate in what I decided — until last year, that is."

"What happened last year?"

A flash of an abortive smile lit her face and was gone. She said, "Last year, I decided to go to Mexico on the spur of the moment."

"You mean you dropped everything and went to Mexico on a whim?" Up to this revelation, I had been impressed with how strictly conscientious she was as she described her most responsible life as a mother, student and employee.

"Well, not exactly," she said with a full smile. "My good friend, Marge, persuaded me to go with her. I struggled with it for a whole day."

"Did your decision create great problems for you?"

"No. It was actually a fantastic vacation. I anticipated the trip with both excitement and worry. The surprise was that the trip exceeded my fondest dreams. It was great fun."

"How do you feel about having been so 'impulsive'?"

"Glad — but guilty. Maybe I should have spent my time and money on something more productive."

"More productive in what way?"

"I don't know. Maybe by going to school, or by spending more time with my kids — something that would have paid off in the long run."

"And is that part of your concern about not completing the MBA?"

"Yes. I'm afraid I'll regret it later if I quit now. How would my family and friends react?"

"Yes, how *would* they react? Would they disown you? Cast you aside?"

"No," she laughed, seeing my point, "They would still love and accept me. It would be hard to tell them, though. My dad always claims one can never get enough education. He had to drop out of high school and he believes 'more is better.' He'd be very disappointed."

"How do you know that?"

"I don't really *know* it, but I think he would."

"So you're struggling with the problem of whether you should be the 'responsible good child' for everybody else, or be the 'impulsive child' and do what *you* want to do?"

"That's about it. I've been trying to do everything on my

list. I have too many irons in the fire, too much for any one person to do."

"We often take on more than we can manage or keep things we could more wisely discard. Each territory, whether it is a relationship, an activity or an actual possession, requires time and effort to maintain. Instead of trying to do it all, maybe you could pick and choose."

"You mean, do a little of all of them?"

"Or choose which ones you will adopt."

"That will take some thought."

"Aside from trying to fulfill what you think are the expectations of other people, what is it that *you* would like to do?"

"Can I be completely selfish? First, I'd love to play more. I'd love to be a part-time student studying French — in France. I'd like to study several foreign languages and travel. And I know I'd rather not complete the MBA."

"As a grownup, the right to make a decision is your territory, and that includes the right to change your mind."

"So, just because I've started something, it doesn't mean I have to finish it?"

"I think it was an inventor who said it was very important to know when to give up an idea."

"I'll think about it. See you next week."

Like Ann, we all have old "duties" which lay claim to our energies, block our spontaneity, and make parts of our lives a joyless drudgery. They are like the clutter in our homes that we have skirted or climbed over so many times we don't realize any longer it is there. These duties have become "command performances" to which we blindly submit. We may grumble about them to others, but we often fail to give ourselves a hearing about those same complaints.

When Ann came in for her next appointment, she looked happier and more relaxed. She said, "I'm not going to clean up my MBA plate. I have a belly full."

She had decided to think about her future and take the time to make another decision.

Do you make you *get up in the morning when you would love to sleep in — and could without any serious* consequence? And when you're on your way to go for a leisurely stroll you've wanted for a long time, and your neighbor asks you to watch her baby for an hour so she can get a facial, do you put aside the stroll? And do you have to get everything done before you relax? Have you guiltily hidden several unfinished projects, promising yourself you will finish them someday? Do you dare throw them all into the trash? Who is in charge here? "DUTY" or you?

Chapter 24.

Privacy in Shared Space

Often we experience times we want to be left alone, but the surroundings seem to make that impossible. A few creative individuals might manage to win some privacy in crowded places, while the rest of us try to tolerate the crowding. For some, the pressure becomes unbearable.

Carla, an elementary school teacher, consulted me. She said, "I'm going to quit. Teaching is not for me after all."

"Why do you think so?"

"I have 24 students this year — probably the best group I've had in my nine years of teaching in this school — ."

"It's the best group ever, but you're ready to quit? What's the problem?"

"Me! I feel like a rubber band that keeps getting stretched further and further. I'm about ready to snap." Tears came to her eyes. "I don't seem to have the energy it takes any more. Some mornings, I dread going to work. And at the end of the day, I'm exhausted."

"Are these feelings new?"

"I loved teaching my first few years. There was lots of joy. But each year seems more difficult than the one before, even though I know the curriculum better and I'm more confident."

"What particular aspect makes the teaching more difficult?"

"I've asked myself that same question over and over again. It's so frustrating because I don't know!"

"Carla, are there specific times of the day when the frustration is most noticeable?"

She thought for a moment and then smiled. "Well, this is embarrassing but the first thing that came to mind was when I was in the bathroom yesterday."

"The bathroom?"

"Yes. The only breaks I get during my day are during lunch and recess, and it really irritated me when one of the teachers followed me into the bathroom and talked nonstop about one of her students."

"Why did that upset you?"

"I'm not sure, but I think it was the intrusion."

"You wanted to be alone, and she violated your privacy?"

"Yes," she said, "It reminded me of the time I was a Junior High School student and I had to take group showers in my physical education classes. I was horribly self-conscious about my developing body so I'd do anything to get out of undressing in front of everybody. I would deliberately forget my PE clothes or I'd get my mother to write me an excuse."

"So both then, during the group showers and in the bathroom yesterday, you felt a loss of privacy?"

"At least at home, when I shut the bathroom door, it means 'Stay Out,' and my children do. If I want some privacy I can disconnect the telephone and go soak in the bathtub."

"Are there other times when you experience unwanted intrusions?"

Another instance came quickly. "Yes, during lunch. Our faculty lounge is small and it's not very quiet. It's also messier than I like. There are posters and announcements scattered all over the room — horribly public."

"We each differ in our appetites for privacy and neatness," I said. "Some need a great deal, others less. In shared spaces, such as our workplaces, it can be difficult to find."

"But those seem like little things to be upset about."

"It's often the little things we try to ignore that become larger problems later. At your workplace, there's no space that is yours alone. You share the space with the rest of the faculty and with the students. *On your home ground you can control the contact with others by shutting doors, closing curtains, or refusing to answer the phone. There, you have many barriers you can use to keep others away. But when you're in shared space, there are few protections for your privacy.*"

"Even now, at the tennis club, I feel uncomfortable undressing and showering in the locker room with others," she admitted. "It seems to me I spend most of my weekdays in shared space. Even my apartment complex is shared with others. So are the roads I drive to get here — the post office, grocery store — even your office!"

"Even my office," I laughed. "And each group controlling the space establishes rules that dictate how you have to behave in that setting. In a church, you have to whisper, but you can yell at the ballpark."

"I know I need more privacy at work than I have," she said. "What can I do to get more? Maybe I should hang a 'Do Not Disturb' sign around my neck."

"You might need to find some similar way to signal to your co-workers that you need solitude."

"Would it be rude or selfish to want to be left alone?"

"No, not at all," I said. "*Some may criticize you, but when we're bunched together on a shared territory it becomes important to develop some signs, as you've suggested, so we can have some badly needed privacy from time to time.*"

"Are you saying that it's my responsibility to protect my privacy?"

"*Yes, that's true of all of our territories. Others will intrude or take over if we don't defend our turf. But the good news is that we usually don't need to fight them off with our fists. A message will often do the trick.*"

"Give me an example."

An illustration came to mind which demonstrates the degree of creativity sometimes required. "I had a friend who would wear a special baseball cap around the house

— her signal to her husband and children that she wanted to be left alone to study for her final examinations in dental school."

"Sounds rather drastic."

"They were crowded in a small house and she had to work out some signal that showed she needed uninterrupted time to study. That meant that the family members had to solve their own problems on their own, get help from someone else or wait until she was available. They all discovered indirect benefits. They found new solutions for old problems."

"As a mother, I'd love that. But I can't wear a baseball cap in the faculty lounge or the bathroom when I want to be left alone."

"Maybe you can find your own way of protecting your privacy."

The next week, Carla telephoned with an update on her situation.

"Hi!" she said, sounding elated. "I've been enjoying some alone time at home and here at school. I take Tuesdays and Fridays during lunch hour to enjoy privacy. I lock the classroom and hang a sign on the door that says, 'Do Not Disturb.' Sometimes, I even go to lunch at a little cafe nearby — by myself. Of course, I had to explain what I was doing to my colleagues. A couple of them thought it was a great idea, and they're doing the same.

"You know what? I'm enjoying teaching again, as much as I used to. I've decided teaching *is* my thing. But — so is solitude."

Many of us have the idea that being with others is always good, and being alone is bad. What we all need is some alone time to rest, recreate, and replenish our energies. Being alone and being with others we care about are both important, but they need to be in rhythm and harmony, alternating like the high and low notes of a melody.

Chapter 25.

Breaking Free

*M*any of us create more problems for ourselves than we realize, by being only "nice," and by not recognizing there are times when we need to be firm, confrontive, assertive or even aggressive. By permitting others to intrude into our territories, we encourage more incursions.

Shannon, a quiet and compliant woman of 32, suffered from chronic headaches and bowel difficulties which her physician thought were signs of emotional stress.

In one of her interviews, she said, "I try to be a good sport. When my mother-in-law comes to visit, she likes to have the turkey done a certain way, and I try to please her. She also likes the house to be neat and clean, so I try to do it the way she wants. She doesn't agree with the way Del and I discipline the children, so she often takes over and handles them. Ten-year-old Archie asked me, 'Do I have to do what Grandma says? She's not my mother.' I told him he had to do what she wanted because she was his granny. He obeyed, but you could tell he was angry about it.

"No matter how hard I try, or how many ways I try to please her, I always seem to fall short. Do you think my headaches come from that?"

"I think your headaches have to do with being angry and not letting it out."

"Well, I do get a little upset with her."

"A `*little upset*'?"

"Sometimes, *a lot.*"

"And what do you do with your `upset'?"

"I can't show her I'm displeased."

"Or *furious?*"

Shannon's face reflected her discomfort with the words and the emotions they identified. For many years, she had progressively bottled up her anger, building up internal pressures. Those pressures were now emerging in her physical symptoms.

As anyone would, Shannon resented anyone's intrusion into her affairs. But she had been reared to be a "nice child" who never misbehaved or showed displeasure. As a child, she had been taught "The Thumper View of Life." In Walt Disney's cartoon, Bambi, Thumper says, "If you can't say something nice, then don't say anything." Shannon had been strictly disciplined to contain and hide any emotion which was unpleasant. As a result, she was now unable to deal with her territorial rights. She was handicapped, as many people are, by childhood training that not only fails to teach proper self assertiveness but forbids normal aggressiveness altogether.

In one of our interviews, she justified her avoidance of unpleasantness. She said, "I don't like to hurt anyone's feelings."

"That's not quite true."

She was startled.

"Actually, you hurt one person very much, most of the time."

She looked confused. Then she smiled. "You mean *me?*"

"Yes. Wouldn't you agree that *it is cruel to treat one person as though she has no right to be angry or aggressive, and force her to kowtow to everyone else?*"

"I never thought of it that way."

"You do believe in equality, don't you?"

"You mean that everyone has a right to equal treatment? Yes, of course I do."

"But then, you're believing in equality while practicing a form of slavery."

After considerable counseling, Shannon learned to accept herself as a person as important as anyone else. And when she accepted her own anger and aggressiveness, as natural aspects of her being, she learned to deal more effectively with other people. She was now ready to face her mother-in-law.

In preparation for her encounter, she reached an understanding with Del that the problem between her and his mother had to be dealt with. She asked him to stay out of their coming struggle, explaining to him that their conflict was a matter which belonged to them. He agreed.

The next time his mother visited, Shannon was preparing the holiday dinner. Her mother-in-law said, "You shouldn't put your turkey in the oven wrapped in foil. That will prevent it from browning."

Shannon, having prepared for this occasion by rehearsing many times before a mirror, said, "Now, Mother. When we're in *your* home, you are the boss. When we're in *my* home, I'm the bosslady, and I get to do things my way. It may not be as good as the way you do it, but I guess I have to learn by my own mistakes. You go out and entertain Bob and Dad. I'll take care of things here."

In what she said, Shannon was clearly marking off her own territory, and recognizing her mother-in-law's domain. By taking the stand and, in her manner of doing so, she showed her confidence, clarity and determination to follow through.

Her mother-in-law said, "Well! *I* know when I'm not wanted."

She got her hat and coat and said, "Henry, we're going home!"

"But we haven't had dinner yet."

"*We* are going home."

Del was very troubled. He tried to persuade his mother to stay, but she was angry and determined.

Shannon said, "I'm sorry you need to go before dinner is served. We'll see you later."

Del's mother was silent.

After his parents left, Shannon served the turkey to Del and herself. Although there was some tension in the air, Shannon seemed strangely pleasant and untroubled.

In describing to me what happened, Shannon said, "I was surprised that I could do it. Afterwards, I had a mixture of feelings. On the one hand, I felt bad in rejecting her help and hurting her feelings, but I also had a good feeling about taking charge of my own life for a change."

Although his mother was miffed, she recovered from it.

Del said, "I was really worried for a while. No one has ever talked to my mother like that. I thought I'd never see her again. She didn't come the next two times Shannon invited them, but they came for my birthday. My mother acted as though nothing had happened. She and Shannon talked to each other the way they always have and, from then on, things between them have been great. Of course, my mother now stays out of the kitchen when Shannon is cooking."

Firmly setting the limits on her own territory that time made it less difficult for Shannon to set boundaries the next time. By making things clear in this way, she did a kindness in the long run both for her mother-in-law and for herself, by making it less likely that they would have greater, and more serious, misunderstandings later.

Shannon's headaches disappeared, and her bowel problems decreased. By being assertive about protecting her domain, she got rid of some needless stress.

All of us need to become more clearly aware of what is our territory and what isn't. We must recognize the boundaries separating them. Then, not only do we need to respect the territories and claims of others, we need to defend our own boundaries when they are threatened. The protection of our territory includes maintaining its integrity against, or breaking free from, the efforts of others who might try to control us. That is another form of the proper care of our own domains and ourselves.

Chapter 26.

Losing Myself

Who *we are is often very much wrapped up in* what *we own. That's something about which we become keenly aware when we are uprooted in moving from one place to another. Placing too much importance on external objects and too little on our internal development can set the stage for trauma.*

Cora, a handsome, silver-haired woman who consulted with me was obviously agitated.

She said, "I don't know why I've suddenly become insecure and dependent. It's so unlike me. Ever since we moved here, three months ago, I have felt ill at ease and discontented. I've never been like this before. My husband, Bruce, is feeling somewhat the same way. We both feel we've made a terrible mistake moving here from California. There, we were comfortable and well established. But Bruce got a business offer he "couldn't refuse," so we sold our home and moved.

"It's even worse with Bruce. He's nervous and upset all the time. He used to be happy and fun. We're thinking seriously of moving back to California, even though there are many things we like here. If we had our own furniture we could begin to feel at home here."

"Your own furniture? I don't understand. Did you get rid of your furniture in California?"

"Oh, no. We lost everything in the fire. The van in which our belongings were being moved caught fire and destroyed everything we owned, except what we had with us."

"When you say, 'everything,' to what are you referring?"

"Our clothes, our furniture, our heirlooms, photo albums, everything. This suit I have on is all I had left. I keep wearing it because it's me. It's the only thing I have that is me. I've bought some new things, but they seem . . . foreign."

I saw her husband the next day. Bruce looked annoyed, but there was also an undercurrent of tension in his speech.

"Did Cora seem angry because I brought us up here from California?"

As psychologists are wont to do, I countered his question with one of mine. Rather than being a meaningless ploy, such tactics are usually aimed to avoid distractions and to focus on more relevant issues.

"Angry? Why would she be angry?"

"Because I seem to have made such a terrible mistake in taking the position up here."

"How was it such a terrible mistake?"

"Neither of us has been happy for a moment since we arrived. Everything seems to be a hardship. I've never been so dissatisfied in my life. The job seems to be all I thought it would be. That's not a problem. The home we're buying seems to be a decent one in a good neighborhood, and it's a lot larger than the same money would have bought in Walnut Creek. We're both out of sorts and don't know why."

Cora and Bruce were experiencing more than the usual amount of stress that people encounter when they make a major move. Since they had undergone counseling previously, they knew they needed to explore more deeply to get to the root of their disturbance.

My inquiries could uncover no significant marital problem, no work problems, relationship difficulties or personality maladjustment. The only other significant factor seemed to be related to the fire and the loss of their belongings.

Before Cora and Bruce left their previous home, they'd had to sort through their belongings and get rid of some of their possessions. As they cleaned the garage, they debated about what should be kept and what should be discarded.

Cora asked Bruce, "Why are you keeping all these magazines?"

Bruce said, "Because there are a lot of good articles about fishing in them that I will want to read sometime."

"When was the last time you read one of them?"

"I don't remember."

"That's because you haven't read any of them for years, and you're not likely to read any in the next ten years."

"Yeah? Well why are you keeping all that knitting stuff in two big boxes? You haven't knitted anything in a long time."

"I plan to do some knitting this winter. I have several projects in mind."

"Sure. Just like last year and the year before. I haven't seen any production yet."

Cora and Bruce were struggling with a recurring problem most of us have from time to time. The reasons we give for keeping our treasures — which our partners often regard as trash, cover every reason but the real ones.

Bruce was a successful engineer, a man who loved to own fine things. He collected expensive fishing gear, high priced sporting goods, and a new fiberglass boat. He sported the latest in hunting and fishing clothes. His identity included his possessions and was heavily dependent upon them. On one occasion, when someone accidentally dented the fender of his new car, he got very angry as if he had been personally slapped. The other driver had to do some fast talking to avoid a fight.

Cora had lived the role of mother-homemaker and had enjoyed it fully. Her two children were now in college, so she was at loose ends. She thought about getting a job, but Bruce didn't approve of the idea, so after a few arguments with him Cora had given it up.

During their move, Cora and Bruce had driven ahead

to wait for the moving van to arrive. They received a telephone call at their motel telling them that the moving van had caught fire, and they would be unable to get their belongings until the following week. Bruce asked whether their things were O.K., but wasn't able to get any information. Later, they learned that the fire completely destroyed everything they had. They were in shock at first, then devastated. They were able to see the burned vehicle, but nothing could be salvaged from the ashes. They bought some new clothes and furniture, but both became depressed and anxious.

Cora said, "It's like my whole history was destroyed. I have no pictures, no clothes, no furniture, nothing. Sometimes I wonder who I am, if I'm still the same person. The clothes I wear aren't me. The house isn't me, and the furniture is all foreign. I've almost completely lost my identity. What am I going to do?"

"Do you and Bruce have family nearby?"

"My mother and father live 300 miles away. Bruce's family are in California."

"It would probably help if they had some photographs of you, Bruce and the children. They could get copies for you.."

Their parents visited them and not only gave them some photographs they had, but also some familiar things from Cora's and Bruce's past, which helped a lot.

She and Bruce struggled through the next weeks and months, reforming their lives. They had truly lost a lot of the supports of their identities, so for a long time they were anxious, in mourning, living with uncertainty. It was only very gradually that they regained some clarity and some stability.

Later, Cora said, "I never realized how fragile an identity can be. I truly lost sight of who I was. It's only now that some time has passed that I again have some reasonable clarity of who I am."

The difference between the impact of giving up her knitting and giving up her intimate belongings was not only in the extent of the loss, but in the connections between who she was and the objects which supported her identity. Photographs are, of course, clearly tied in with identity, but so are clothes and furniture. Another factor was in her unreadiness to part with the objects that were burned.

In one of her interviews, Cora said, "I felt a little like I had when our two children left home to go to college. I was lost. It was as if I were no longer a mother. I didn't have a place. I didn't have a meaning. It was only after a few months in my new job that I began feeling I was somebody who belonged somewhere."

"Which of the two experiences, the children's leaving or the aftermath of the burned moving van, bothered you the most?"

She pondered for a moment. "Strangely enough, the loss of our clothes and things was more disturbing. I had concentrated on preparing my young people to leave the nest, so that I was almost ready to let them go when they went. And I knew they'd be back.

"With the fire, it was different. Everything that told me who I was and how I was, had disappeared and it wasn't ever coming back. I had to build from scratch."

Most of us don't have to face such extreme trauma, but we do have times when we must let go of some territory and move on. If we anticipate it, and prepare for it, it is much easier. The losses have the most powerful assault on the identity of those who place too much reliance on external supports, and the least impact on those who have more fully developed the richness of their internal selves.

When we move our place of residence, it is always extremely disturbing. We might think we are merely homesick, or that we only miss our friends and relatives. But an important part of our disturbed feelings has to do with our being habit-forming creatures, and with our attachment to our physical surroundings. *The expression, "There's no place like home" is literally true. Over time, we have built up millions of little habits that depend for their completion on the environments we are in and many of those habits are tied in with our nests.* When we move, we are stuck with those millions of habitual actions that depended for their completion, the sights, sounds and movements, colors, smells and the people of the old environment. Those now frustrated habits compound our difficulties.

Adele luxuriated in the balmy sunshine of her deck, musing about her good fortune: the children were all successfully launched in lives and families of their own, her house remodeling was finally finished, and she could now relax and enjoy it all.

That was before Howard came home and peeked around the door at her with an uncomfortable look on his face. "Hi, honey." The attempt at being casual was a failure.

"What is it?"

He struggled to find the right words, but couldn't locate them in their usual places.

"C'mon. Out with it. I know something's on your mind — wherever you've left it."

With effort, the words came, "We have to move."

"You're joking, aren't you?" She knew he wasn't.

He didn't bother to answer.

"When?"

"Thirty days."

The surface remained calm, but a flood of despair overtook her. She couldn't muster a tear. She got up, dressed and said she had to go shopping for some groceries.

After 12 years of stability, the first she'd known in the 23 years of their marriage, it was to be on the road again, business nomads. First, it was the military, with its multiple moves, which wasn't all bad because Europe had been a delightful experience. Then the transfers after Howard rose to be a manager. She'd taken the moves in stride at first, but began to hate them. Then as a Vice President, he could at last put some roots down.

She pushed the grocery cart absentmindedly down the aisle. She thought, "I can do it." Then,

"*But I don't want to!*"

The man ahead of her turned to look at her. She was as startled as he was. She didn't bother to smile or explain.

Many people move from place to place in our highly mobile society. Although they seem to take it in stride, and

even to enjoy it at times, it is always stressful. It was especially wrenching for Adele.

In the month before they left, she consulted with me.

She said, "I'm done swallowing my feelings and being a
good martyr. I'm going to let my emotions out so I can look
at them, and then I'll decide what I'm willing to do."

"I'm not all that sure I'm going to go with Howard. I've
thought seriously about letting him go by himself, and have
him commute back here whenever he can. I've just started
a job that I like, and if it weren't for the fact that it's only
part time, Howard and I would have a real rhubarb about
moving."

"What makes it most difficult for you?"

"I guess it's the first time in my life that I've been me. Until the past few years, I've only been Howard's wife, his
helpmate, his assistant. But now, I have an identity of my
own. I'm a full fledged person in my own right, with my own
opinions, my own feelings, and my own way of doing and
seeing things. What I'm afraid of is that I'll lose a lot of that.
Going back to the way it was is totally unacceptable to me
now."

"What makes you think you would lose it all?"

"Just moving is going to destroy a lot. I have to leave
my friends. I'll be so far away that I can't come back so
easily. And a big part of it is that I've finally been able to
have my own nest. We moved into an old home that
needed some work. I've put my own blood, sweat and
tears into it, and it's the first time I have my own place. It's
me. To lose it all will kill me."

"It may not be necessary for you to *lose* it all. There may
be other ways of dealing with the problems."

"I've thought of that, but I can't see any way of keeping two homes."

"You might find a way."

Being a very creative and dynamic woman, she put her
mind to the task and eventually arrived at some solutions
she could live with. She had a talk with her sister and decided that she would rent her home to her sister for five
years, after which she and Howard would return, with or
without the company's agreement or his job.

She'd found a way to put her home on the shelf, and keep that precious piece of territory available for the future. Giving it up would have felt like putting one of her children up for adoption. It had become a part of her identity. It expressed her ideas, feelings and spirit. Keeping her nest in storage allowed her to move with less trauma.

In one of her interviews with me, she said, "I hate to be selfish about this, but I've invested so much of myself in my home, in living here, and with my friends."

"That's being selfish?"

"Yes, of course. I should be like most wives and pack it up and live with it."

"And be a good slave?"

"Somehow, I feel guilty not doing that, and yet I feel I have a right to take care of my own needs, too."

"It sounds like you're torn between treating yourself fairly, and treating yourself like a person who doesn't deserve consideration."

"I thought I'd mastered that one, yet here I am doing the same thing I lived with for so many years. I guess I need to get a refresher course."

She came to realize quite clearly that her stands with Howard about the home and moving back, weren't the irrational, selfish choices she half-felt they were. She also saw that she didn't have to abandon her friends altogether. She would return for visits from time to time, as often as she needed to and could afford. She would give herself the gift of reunion with them, because that would be what she would want for her best friend, and she had resolved to be her own best friend. Beyond that, she decided to telephone her relatives and good friends when she needed to.

Knowing this, Adele took my advice and devoted a lot of attention and energy during the first weeks of her days in Chicago to establishing new routines, developing new habits, new ways for old patterns to find some completion. She did many things the way she had done them in her former home, and deliberately set up new routines for those habits which required them. That eased the transition for her.

On a brief visit, she arranged for a short appointment. She said, "Thanks for reminding me to take care of myself. I needed that. I was getting caught up in my old, bad slavery habits.

"We're established there in Chicago, and I'm doing very well, because I decided to make the best of it for my stay. I've found a part time job in kitchen and bathroom design, and I'm having a ball with it. When we get back here, I'm going to have myself a career to nurse. I've discovered that I was ready to embark on a new tangent in life, and moving came at the right time to help me find what I want to do for the next 50 years."

She had weathered the crisis by softening many of the adjustments, and not severing all her connections completely, as she first thought she might have to do.

We can learn the way to cope from our youngsters. Many children form an adhesive attachment to some piece of their environment which is a source of comfort under stress. That tattered remnant of a blanket, the much patched and otherwise repaired teddy bear or the piece of ribbon and the much-sucked thumb have almost magical powers to comfort the child. They are there, even when the security providing parents are gone, and make a symbolic substitute until they return. As adults, we, too, need something to provide a sense of comfort at times.

Moving is never free of stress, but it doesn't have to be traumatic. We will all invest some of our energies in our physical environment, and we will establish habits with parts of it, so that separation from our old environments will necessarily hurt. But like the child with his "Binky," if we can take with us most of what is precious, the pain will be less. What is most precious, of course, is our inner core, our identity.

Chapter **27.**

Childhood Rules for Adult Living

*M*any things in life are useful for specific purposes or for a given period of time. But if they are used incorrectly, they may do damage. One of those tools is masking tape, used to keep paint off other painted surfaces. If allowed to remain too long, it adheres to the paint it covers and, when removed, damages the surface it was originally supposed to protect.

Another of those things is the body of childhood rules. Parents teach their children many things, and one of the most important is the group of guidelines for behavior. Those rules have a most valuable function for the young individual and for society. They train individuals to function in a civilized society. But, like masking tape, if those rules are employed too long, they do damage.

For example, Claudia, a conscientious homemaker, stopped in the middle of her housecleaning one day and, with a determined look, abandoned the bucket and brush in the middle of the floor and discarded her apron. She changed into her bikini and lay in the sun, reading her new magazine. Five minutes into her tan, after much internal squirming and physical restlessness, she angrily threw down the magazine, and went back to her scrubbing. Her new resolution had evaporated as quickly as a summer sprinkle.

But, after fifteen minutes of frantic scouring, she hurled the brush at the kitchen wall. She went to the cupboard and began throwing dishes at the same wall, raging and cursing as they crashed and shattered. She suddenly stopped and slumped to the floor, sobbing.

In her first interview with me, she said, "I don't know why I can't enjoy the sun after a week of clouds. What's wrong with that? After all, I work hard. You'd think I deserved a little enjoyment. But somehow, I feel so guilty."

Some of us are like Claudia, unable to enjoy ourselves even briefly unless "everything is done." As children, we were taught that we first had to finish our work and then we could play.

Claudia was trying to free herself from the rules she had learned in childhood so she could live like an adult. Her situation is a common one, suffered by many people who aren't clear that their selves and their values are their property. *They are behaving as if some external authority dictates their actions. But that "outside force" is a part of their domain, rules they learned as children. And, as part of their territory, it is subject to their control.*

For example, Claudia had been taught, *"Don't think of yourself; always think of the other person."* That notion helps children to learn to be unselfish and caring. But, if an adult lives by that principle, it becomes a prescription for slavery. Claudia, by thinking only of other people's interests, and never considering her own, often deprived herself.

She had failed to modify the rule to fit her present life. If she had modified it, the rule would read, "You are as important as other people. It is your responsibility to look to your own happiness and satisfactions. In order to do that you will need to be reasonable and considerate of other people, and deal with yourself in a loving, fair way."

The childhood rules are primarily for socialization. *They are poorly suited for guiding adult living, yet some people try to live their adult lives by those principles. Like most things of childhood, as we grow up, we need to leave some of them behind and adapt others for living life as an adult.*

That doesn't mean that all we learned needs to be jetti-

soned, but only that some rules need to be adapted to adult demands. Life for an adult is much more complicated than the life of a child, and the simple rules we learned as children are inadequate for dealing with complexities. Part of the cultivation of our self territory is the process of bringing ourselves up to date with the realities in which we live.

In one interview, Claudia asked, "O. K., so now I know I've been dominated by my childhood rules. How can I free myself from them?"

"First, you need to be able to know when they're present. They all advertise their presence by telling you what you *should, ought, must or have to do*, or what you *shouldn't, ought not or can't do.* If you comply — or if you rebel against them — you are giving them your control.

"Whenever you are dealing with one of them, you need to challenge it, question it, and then *make your own decision as an adult about what is a reasonable and appropriate thing for you to choose to do this time.* You must be in charge of your own life instead of passively submitting to the childhood rules."

"But I have done that. The next thing that happens is that I feel terribly guilty for not doing the 'right thing.'"

"For the first few times, you may feel guilty. But if you have truly considered your course of action and are doing what is reasonable and appropriate for you to do, those feelings will gradually pass. Whenever you feel guilty, ask yourself, 'Am I deliberately doing something to harm anyone else?' If your answer is yes, then your guilt feelings are warranted. Most of the time your answer will be in the negative, and then you need to use your best judgment in making a decision."

"But what if I make a mistake, and what I thought was reasonable, turns out not to be?"

"What do you do most of the time when you make a mistake?"

"I guess I go back to the drawing board and start over."

"That sounds reasonable."

Over the next few weeks Claudia was able to follow through and gradually modify her childhood rules. She found that she could make her own decisions, and she could live her own life. Progressively, she found she felt less and less inappropriate guilt.

In one of her next interviews, Claudia came in feeling depressed. She said, "I did a terrible thing. My aunt Sophie was showing me an antique music box that has been in the family for generations. It was a very special heirloom to her. I accidentally dropped it and broke a corner off. I could tell by the look on her face that it nearly killed her. That was such stupid, careless thing to do. I don't know what I can do about it."

"What did she say about it?"

"She knew I felt bad, so she said it was O.K. She could get it repaired, as she knew a restorer who does fine work with antiques. She said I could pay for the repairs if I wanted to. *If I wanted to!* My God! I'd do anything if it hadn't happened. I'm so clumsy. How could I do such a dumb thing?"

"Why are you so angry with yourself?"

"Wouldn't you be?"

"You deliberately dropped it to hurt her, is that it?"

"Of course not. It slipped out of my hands."

"If your best friend had dropped it, what would you have said to her?"

Claudia had difficulty focusing on my question because she was so wrought up by her feelings. I repeated the question two more times, pressing her to deal with it.

"I guess I would say to her, 'I know you feel terrible. It was an accident. The best thing you can do is remedy it as best you can.'"

"Why would you comfort her? Why wouldn't you tell her she was a stupid, clumsy oaf?"

She looked at me in wonderment that I could ask such an inane question. "Because she would feel so awful about it already. I wouldn't want her to feel worse."

"But it's O.K. for you to torment you, and call yourself names, when you already feel bad? That's what an enemy would do to you. You could be understanding and compassionate with your best friend, but not with you? I think that's being very cruel."

In a follow-up interview, two months later, she came in looking quite different from those first interviews. Her face no longer showed the tension lines, and her radiant smile reflected her mastery over her problems.

She said, "I want you to know that, before I got ready to come here this afternoon, I took a break from my housecleaning and sunned myself for a half hour. And instead of being guilty, angry or frustrated, I feel very good."

Chapter 28.

Yin and Yang

The Chinese symbols or terms, Yin and Yang, represent many opposites. Much of our world seems to be made up of opposites: light and dark, male and female, birth and death and positive and negative. Most leaves have two similar sides. So do most animals. Our muscles are organized so that one set extends our arm, another pulls it in.

Our emotional life is often organized in opposites, but most of us are unaware of this because we convince ourselves that we feel only one emotion at a time. The beginning of this self deception begins very early.

When Sue returned from the hospital with her new baby, she felt hurt when four-year-old Kevin avoided looking at the infant and walked away to the next room to sulk for an hour. Sue made many overtures before he finally gave her a reluctant smile.

During the next few weeks, Sue tried to include Kevin in taking care of the baby, hoping to get him to be a nice big brother to her. One day, Kevin brought his sister's rattle and threw it into the crib, striking her on the nose. As Sue comforted the crying infant, she said, "Kevin, you mustn't throw the rattle so hard. You hit her in the face." Kevin flushed, but he only hung his head and looked at the floor.

Had Sue been more aware of Kevin's feelings, she might have handled the situation very differently. A child in his situation, having been an only child, and the major focus of his parents' attention and then being suddenly demoted, is bound to have feelings of resentment. Much of the territory he once had to himself, has now been removed and given to a little intruder.

The scolding he got from his mother confirmed his lesser status. He needed the correction, but he also needed reassurance of his continuing importance and the love of his mother.

Having a new baby is a heavy burden, as well as a joy to most mothers. It is difficult to have enough energy to meet the necessary demands. It takes even more to minister to the needs of other members of the family. Having so many demands on her, she can easily neglect the displaced child at times.

Even though most parents understand the ambivalence of a child in Kevin's situation, they sometimes behave as if they didn't.

When Kevin said, "I hate her!" Sue told him, "No, you don't. You love her. She's your baby sister."

Sue was denying Kevin's natural resentment and trying to convince him and herself that he "really" loved the baby.

Children who get training like that become adults who subscribe to the notion that we have only one emotion at a time. Instead of learning more about the nature of this part of their identity territory, such individuals are confused about emotions.

Before Kevin would be able to invest positive interest in the baby, he would first have to have some satisfaction of his own needs. Sharing comes after having a sense of belonging and the security of knowing he is valued in his own right.

Sue, and most people, remain unaware that they have ambivalent or mixed feelings. Only rarely do they recognize it, as they are so busy trying to discover which *one* of their feelings they are "really" experiencing.

To solve ambivalence problems, we need to recognize

both of the opposites, and weigh the reasons in each. Then we need to make a decision based on consideration of both of them. If we truly make a decision, we will be able to live with the consequences. But if we find ourselves fretting about our choice, or flip-flopping, we have "copped out" again.

And, if Sue had been able to do it, she might have been able to recognize that she, too, had mixed emotions about parenting. For example, she would see that she loved being a mother to a little baby, *and* that she some-times resented the bother and burden. She wouldn't have to pretend that she only liked it. Or she would see that her loving Kevin was compatible with being angry with him, re-senting him or even wishing he'd never been born. She could then have understood Kevin's resentment of the new intruder, as well as his budding interest in and caring for his baby sister. She could have helped him accept his own feelings of both curiosity and resentment.

After Sue became more aware of Kevin's feelings, she handled a similar situation differently.

One day, Kevin was feeling neglected. Petulantly, he said, "I didn't want a *girl* baby."

Sue stopped what she was doing, picked Kevin up and put him in her lap, hugging and kissing him. "Sometimes, maybe you wish you didn't have a baby sister at all?"

Kevin nodded.

"Sometimes I feel that way, too. I get tired of having her around. Let's you and I just leave her here in her crib, and go have some ice cream. Would you like that?"

While he was eating, Kevin looked up at Sue, "Some-times, I like Michelle."

Being the complicated creatures we all are, it is prob-ably never true that we are motivated by a single impulse or that we experience only one emotion at a time. In every-thing we do, we have many feelings and urges. Fortunately, even though we are full of mixed feelings and emotions, they usually fall into one of two categories: one for, one against. The Yin and Yang are present in almost everything we do. We are like the old comedian, Jimmy Durante, who used to sing, "Sometimes I get the feeling that I want to go.

. . and then I get the feeling that I want to stay." In a word, we are *ambivalent.*

This ambivalence is the basis for conflict. When the two desires or motives are evenly balanced, we appear "wishy-washy." We might start out one way, then reverse direction. We might do this again and again.

When we want so strongly to have only one emotion that we ignore the incompatible ones, we are deceiving ourselves. To put feelings aside doesn't get rid of them any more than ignoring storm warnings will eliminate the coming storms.

If we are angry with someone and try to ignore those feelings and show only our friendly ones, the anger will continue to emerge in spite of our efforts to deny and conceal it. Others will sense the anger and think us "phony" or insincere.

Even when one side of the conflict is much stronger than the other, the opposition is still there.

Caught in conflict between contradictory pushes, we try to resolve the issue by siding with one and ignoring the other. But the rejected one will not be ignored.

We may fool ourselves for a while by trying to force a choice of one, using "will power," for instance. But those of us who have been on a diet know how that works. We vow to diet, and try to ignore the opposing wishes to eat. We use our "will power," but our "won't power" refuses to be denied. It comes back with a vengeance in an eating binge.

It's very much like a parent who favors only one child and ignores another. The ignored one will make the parent pay for that neglect. Siding with one of two opposing forces doesn't work either. Ignoring one of them only makes it more forceful as it accumulates strength the longer it is denied.

To solve the problem, we need to recognize both of the opposites, and weigh the reasons for each. Then, like Sue, we need to make a decision based on consideration of both of them.

Sue came to see not only her love and enjoyment of her children, but also that she felt the need to escape from the burdens and turmoil from time to time. She recognized that Kevin's resentment existed side by side with his genuine caring and enjoyment of Michelle. She learned to deal with all of the feelings, giving each its place, helping Kevin to accept his own feelings of both curiosity and resentment.

Like Yin and Yang, the two sides of an issue are part of a whole.

Chapter 29.

Pandora's Box

Pandora was a Greek goddess. Jupiter gave her a box, which she was to present to the man who married her. When the box was opened, "all the evils that flesh is heir to," flew out.

One interpretation of this could be that, because people are always fearful of something new, they too hastily judged the things that came out of the box as "evils." As they discovered the nature of the contents, they found vast riches and benefits. After all, the name, Pandora, means "All-gifted."

In a sense, each living organism has a Pandora's Box full of riches: latent talents, potentials, possibilities and endowments. The tiny seed, which becomes a beautiful flower, contains that potential. The riches that humans contain are vastly more complex and can be cultivated, honed, developed and nurtured into enormously complicated forms. Sometimes, we are frightened of what we discover, as something we learn about ourselves is so strange. But at other times, the things we learn about our inner nature can be not only remarkable, but powerful and beneficial for us.

For example, Dawn was little aware of the contents of her own psyche. In her first interview, she said, "I need you to help me get along. I never seem to be able to learn as quickly as other people and my thinking is always a bit strange."

"Tell me what you think is strange about your thinking."

"Well, what I think always seems to be different than what other people think."

"Give me an example of what you mean."

She paused for a few seconds, then said, "I was thinking of moving to a different apartment, but my brother, Denny, and my sister-in-law thought that was foolish. They said it would be farther away from where I work, so that wouldn't be sensible."

"But did you have some other reasons why you wanted to move?"

"I wanted to be closer to my friend, Nadia, who lives on the South Side."

"And you felt that would be more important than having to drive a little further to work?"

She nodded. "There was another reason. I wanted to move farther away from Denny. He and his wife, Caroline, tend to supervise me a lot. They like me to spend a lot of my free time with them. They're good to me, and spend a lot of money on me, but I'd like to be able to get away by myself now and then."

"Give me another example of how your thinking seems to be strange."

"My dad thinks I shouldn't be wasting my time working in a warehouse. He says it's a man's job, and it's dangerous besides."

"So why are you working there?"

"I like it. There's no end of challenge. I'm pretty strong, and I can do any work the guys there can do. Besides, I get to run the forklifts, and sometimes I help the dispatcher organize the shipments."

"It sounds to me as though you're saying that, if you don't think the way your family does, your thinking is 'strange.' Is that it?"

"They're usually right."

"And you're not?"

"Sometimes, because I'm not as smart as they are."

"What do you mean, you're not as smart?"

"Well I've always been slow. My dad thinks I'm a bit retarded."

Her last statement was startling. She was clearly not retarded, and her thinking was quite clear. I began to think members of her family used ideas about her being 'strange' or 'retarded,' to control her. To get some of these notions out of our way, I gave Dawn an intelligence test. The results showed that she was of superior intelligence, in the upper 10% of the population! But, even after seeing those results, it took several weeks before she began to change her mind about being retarded.

Dawn had a tendency to play the clown, and to act like a naive child.

In one interview, she was clowning and laughing about having been mistakenly criticized by one of her supervisors, who didn't know someone else had been responsible for an error.

"You're laughing and joking, but I think you're upset by what happened. It's as though you're telling me you're stupid, and I'm supposed to believe that. You and I both know you're not stupid. Why didn't you stand up for yourself and tell the supervisor you didn't make the mistake?"

She blushed. "It's O.K. I'm used to taking the blame."

"No, I don't think it is O.K., and neither do you. You know, Dawn, you can be pretty cruel."

She was startled.

"You let somebody take the flack for something she didn't do, and you don't even stand up for that person."

"Well, it's just me, so it's O.K."

"'*Just me*,' so it doesn't matter? You're telling me *you* don't matter. I think that's terrible. You ought to be ashamed treating a person like that."

That was the beginning of Dawn's awareness of how badly she treated herself. Gradually she learned that merely thinking she was fair minded wasn't enough. *Believing in equality of persons had to be put into practice for it to mean anything, and she had to deal with herself as well as she treated anyone else to be consistent. In a way, she was prejudging and dealing with herself as an unworthy person. And since she was with her self 24 hours a day, she was potent in undermining any good feelings she could have.*

Part of her therapy was in getting her to look at herself more objectively, and treating herself in a loving, fair way. *Again, she discovered* the necessity for action. *Only when she treated herself in kind, considerate ways did she feel worthy.* As she came to accept herself as an intelligent person, she had less need to behave in an immature manner.

In her inward searches she discovered, in her Pandora's Box, a host of valuable resources. She learned that she had acquired a great deal of understanding of other people, and that she had developed many social skills, without being aware she had done so. She became curious about learning new things, and considered going back to school, but the idea that she was stupid still remained in the background.

She said, "I guess my father had good reason to think I was retarded. I had a lot of difficulty in school. He used to beat me with a switch when I got bad grades. I remember he used to make me sit down with him and go over my homework. I was so stupid, he'd get frustrated and shout at me."

"You were 'so stupid'?"

She smiled. "Well, *he* thought I was."

"And you played it to the hilt?"

She laughed. "I guess I did."

"So you're not stupid?"

"No. I'm not stupid."

"But, apparently, it was a good weapon to beat your father with?"

"I guess it was."

"You and your father fought each other a lot."

"I never thought of that as fighting. But if I think of him trying to make me learn, and my acting 'retarded,' I can see that we were fighting."

"One of the few ways a child can fight an adult."

"Yes."

"And that kind of fighting is a loving thing to do for oneself."

She puzzled over that one for a while, and gradually came to realize that anger could be an expression of caring when it was used to protect herself from abusive parenting.

She had learned to regard her thinking as 'strange,' but now, began to realize it was her independent thinking which was, for her, even more sensible than others' notions of how she should live her life. She came to trust her own thinking instead of relying so much on what others thought.

Dawn's family had devoted a lot of time and energy guiding and forming her attitudes about herself. In effect, they were intruding into her self territory and defining it as they saw fit, no matter how poorly their constructions served Dawn. Dawn had become confused about her nature, her talents and her efforts, as she allowed other people to tell her about them instead of examining and testing them to see for herself what they were.

Many months later, she said, "It's amazing to me that I let people run me and my life the way I did. It was as though I was an absentee landlord for myself. Other people used me and formed me any way they wanted to and I stupidly . . ."

"Stupidly . . .?"

" . . .*Negligently* . . . let them.

"I'm finding that, as I learn more about myself, there is more to me, and more that I can do with my interests, abilities and capacities. And the more I polish what I have, the more enjoyment and fulfillments I can have."

She had chosen to work in a warehouse because she learned she was competent to do the physical and mental labor required. But as she continued the work, she was encouraged to take on other tasks when others found her to have many good abilities.

She said, "Dad won't let go. He keeps telling me I should be doing something besides working in a warehouse. But I've learned a lot and I've found I have real talent for organization. I spend some time working with the manager and the accountant, so I have a lot of interesting things to do at work."

"So some of your ideas aren't so strange after all?"

"No. They're only different. And they're mine — and they're O.K."

"You seem to have discovered a lot of interesting things in your Pandora's Box."

"Yes, and the more I discover, the more fun I have and the more I find I can do. I think I still have a long way to go, but I have made good progress."

After a pause, she added, "I'm feeling so good, I'd like to try things on my own for a while. Could I call you if I need you?"

She terminated, as many people do, to work on her own. In our kind of work, there is no "cure." There are only improvements and resolutions of problems.

One afternoon, a year later, I received an urgent call from Dawn. She asked if I could see her. When she came in, it was obvious that she was acutely disturbed.

"I thought I was doing so well, and then the whole world fell in on me."

"What happened?"

"Dad knew a man who was a regional manager for a large cosmetics company. He and the man were talking recently, and the regional manager offered to take me on as his assistant, and at a very good salary. Dad was sure it was a great opportunity for me, and more along the lines he thought I should be pursuing. He gave the man complete assurance that I would take the position. He went out on a limb.

"When I told Dad I was happy where I was and that I didn't want to leave, he blew up. He said he always knew I was stupid and would never amount to anything. He stormed out.

"I went to Denny's and Caroline's and told them the story. I should have known better. Denny scolded me and told me Dad was right, and that I probably blew the best opportunity I'd ever have. Caroline agreed with him and suggested I might be able to get in touch with Dad and tell him I'd changed my mind."

"But what is it that *you* want to do?"

"I don't know, now. Maybe I did blow it."

"When you talked with your father, it sounded like you knew what you wanted to do."

"I did, but after I talked with Denny and Caroline, I began to think they were right."

"And your ideas were 'strange'?"

She laughed.

"So what does *Dawn* want to do?"

"I still want to stay where I am and do what I'm doing."

"You're sure?"

"I'm sure."

As she rose to leave, she said, "You know, it's frightening how easily I can lose sight of me."

"Yes, but you can also recapture you. It takes constant effort to keep track of who, how, where and what you are. Becoming you is a full time occupation and will never be done. That's the greatest adventure you'll ever have."

Two years later, when the manager was ill, Dawn took over his responsibilities and implemented several new ideas that made for greater streamlining of the warehouse procedures. Dawn asked for and got, not only a raise, but the position as manager when the manager was unable to return to work.

She called me to tell me the news.

"I finally made it."

"You mean the promotion?"

"Yes, I got that, too. No, I meant that Dad finally accepted the idea that I have my own competent mind, that I am good at what I'm doing, even if it isn't what he thought I should be doing. Today, he said, 'Dawn, I've been wrong. You were right. You kept at what you believed in, and you've proven yourself. I'm really proud of you.' Now, that's a lot. I never expected to hear that. But even more important, I now believe in me a lot more, and I'm proud of me.

"I wonder what else I'll find in Pandora's Box."

195

Epilogue

The world of knowledge is so rich most of us will only scratch the surface of all that is available, particularly scientific knowledge. Much of what exists is written in technical language, so that it might as well be written in hieroglyphics. And yet, some of that knowledge is so useful, it needs to be translated into ordinary language so wo can all benefit from it.

Fortunately, there are among us some translators, as it were, who make some of those "hieroglyphics" understandable and do so in such beautiful and interesting ways, their work is entertaining as well as informative. Robert Ardrey is one of those translators who shared with us a good deal of the information having to do with territoriality in his book, *The Territorial Imperative*. Although most of the studies he cited were done with animals, Ardrey saw how important the basic ideas were to understanding human behavior. His book created quite a sensation in 1966, but, since then, people seem to have forgotten about his ideas. That may have been because they didn't know how useful they could be or what to do about them.

In our work as counselors with people struggling with problems, we have found the concepts of territoriality to be most useful, not only in understanding, but also in the solution of problems. Although the basic notions are quite simple, seeing how they operate in human interaction, and applying the ideas to resolve difficulties, takes a bit of effort and practice. One of the values of the concepts is their broad application to almost all human relationships, to lovers, families and communities.

In the preceding chapters, we have illustrated the many ways in which we all express our needs to have, to control or to acquire more territory, and how our efforts are contested by others. In this closing chapter, we will review territorial concepts and how they apply in life.

Humans, like most animals, are territorial beings. That means that such creatures acquire a certain space or thing and behave as if they "own" it, occasionally leaving markers to show their ownership. Such tenants try to repel trespassers or intruders who violate the sanctity of that belonging. Sometimes the territory is jointly held by two or more individuals, and occasionally that territory will be subdivided into "private," "shared" and "public" areas or spaces. When there is ambiguity about ownership, individuals or groups may contest each other, leading to friction, or even outright warfare, for the holdings.

Almost all conflicts between people are *territorial disputes.* The contenders are attempting to take control over some territory which both parties want or claim.

One way to discover whether someone *owns* a particular territory is to watch how a person or group behaves toward it. Defense of the space or thing shows that someone has a sense of ownership about it. But that doesn't mean that we can't, shouldn't or are forbidden to intrude or contest the ownership. And it doesn't mean that the individual's or group's claim must be accepted. It is prudent, however, to know what we are doing and what the circumstances are.

There are territories that are open to be claimed or used. There are others, over which someone may be claiming ownership, which can be contested. And some territory is legally defined and sanctioned by a larger group (e.g., City, State or Nation) as owned or controlled by some parties, and the larger group will defend those rights.

Some special territories are defined by law as "belonging to" an entity for a given time, and changes in such control are also defined by law. These could be public offices, where the rules of election and change of tenant are strictly governed by the larger group. Here, competition for the tenancy is open and sanctioned, but hedged about with rules. But, even with those restrictions, there is much deviation from them at times by some competitors.

Most of the frictions that arise in contests for control, however, occur in private life, where the rules are vague, subject to our individual interpretation and changeable.

Those of us who have moved to a new city, and sat in "the wrong pew" at church, quickly became aware that someone had staked out some private space in a public setting. We recognize such "squatter's rights" not only in church, but in libraries, lines at the gasoline service station, lines to movies or to have our child chat with Santa Claus at the local department store.

Most animals have a much easier time of it, as their territories are simpler and more obvious. In most cases, animal territories are spatial in nature. Even fish, in their liquid medium, have areas they lay claim to and fight over.

The problem with human territories is their complexity. Not only do we claim space, we also try to acquire and control abstract notions such as "my ideas," "my turn," or "my rights." Even when our territories deal with physical space, human issues are more complicated.

When we drive down a highway, we take possession of a piece of space in front, in back and on both sides of our car — which moves along the highway with us. If someone cuts in too close or "tailgates," we get defensive or "nervous" because we feel someone is infringing on our space.

Sometimes the territories don't move, but the boundaries around them shift. When we talk about ourselves, "I" or "me" can refer to my physical body, or it can mean a psychological space known as my "identity." Then again, it could mean as I once was, or the person I may be in the future. "My home," "my neighborhood," "my country" and "my universe" encircle very different amounts of space.

Another factor, making it difficult to "see" territories, is that each of us has our own unique way of defining what is ours. In essence, the territory concerned can be a psychological entity, defined in people's minds. No two persons' notions of space or belonging are alike. When we don't recognize this, we might try to get someone to "be reasonable" and change their ideas to be like ours. We then become like the *Blind Men and the Elephant,* as we try to convince each other that our own perceptions are right and theirs are wrong.

As children grow up, they need and take more and more territory. That is the cause of great boundary disputes between parents and their children, especially when it comes to the questions of "who has the right to do which, with what and to whom." One person's understanding of those rights may be quite different from another's. Those conceptions can also change with growth and development. Since children are less powerful and less knowledgeable than grownups they must find ways to escape the control of others at times. Deviating from norms and demands, without creating giant disturbances, is an art that children discover can be done innocently, passively or in secret. Rebellious seizure of decision-making territory is a normal aspect of growing up. It may be an effort to escape from what they experience as the stifling control of parents.

Grownups, who live in close relationship with each other, sometimes feel excessively influenced or "controlled" by their partners. Sometimes their accumulated need to be free of such effect reaches the point where they feel compelled to differ with their partner's ideas even when they basically agree with them. At those times, a neighbor's thoughts seem more reasonable — whether they are or not.

When anyone tries to modify our territories, in any way, we will be defensive and protect our owned entity, whether it be our yards or homes, our "lifestyles," our political beliefs or our tastes. All of us naturally resent others treading into our territory, "reading our minds" by telling us what we think or what our attitudes are. We very much mind it when someone "minds our business, our territory," and that is as it needs to be. Those of us who don't properly protect what is ours may lose it, have it abused or stolen. Proper self defense requires that we know how to use our natural aggressiveness, and that we have developed appropriate skills in using the energy in a constructive way.

Our territories and their boundaries require a certain

"optimum distance" between us and anyone else. If some-one exceeds that distance, young moderns are likely to tell them to "Get out of my face!" That distance is less with those we know and like, and greatest with strangers. It is also greater when we are tired or angry. We need to be left alone then. But when we are secure, comfortable, and in a good mood, we need and can accept closeness.

Many people believe that intimacy and togetherness are always desirable and good. But there is a limit to the amount and degree of closeness we can tolerate. Every-one needs time to be alone, free from the pressure of oth-ers, to rest and recuperate. At other times, we will need closeness and togetherness. There is a natural rhythm be-tween those needs. When that rhythm is disturbed, by forc-ing closeness when we need alone time, it is irritating. Indi-vidual needs for togetherness and alone time are also dif-ferent for each person, and also different from time to time.

Because of these factors, it isn't easy to locate the boundaries of another person as they are at any given mo-ment. Asking for Information from those we deal with can be very important. With strangers, it is even more true. That is why we engage in "small talk" with people we don't know. "Small talk" is a series of probes to discover where the boundaries are and what the nature and condition of the territory is.

Aggression and Conflict

Aggression is necessary to acquire territory, to define its boundaries and to retain control over it. Most of us have been trained not to be aggressive, as it has been defined to be bad, hurtful and destructive. But aggressive drive is a natural and necessary component of our biological makeup, and it has a necessary and important role in our lives.

Aggression is basic in the defense of our territories, and conflict with others is inevitable, not only because others in-trude into our space, but also because differences in defini-tion of what belongs to whom always exists.

The closer our relationship with others, the more territo-ries are shared and overlap, so that boundaries are blurred and contention arises. This is why there is more frequent and more intense conflict between people who are closer to one another than between strangers.

Sometimes conflict can serve a valuable function. It can clarify boundaries. Aggression is necessary to maintain the integrity and clarity of our identity boundaries and to keep meddlers out. More constructive and less wearing, when it is adequate to the task, is negotiation.

Identity

One territory we all have is called by various names: I, myself, me, the kind of person I am, my individuality, my identity. The clearer we are about the boundaries, and the better we know the territory within, the more secure and confident we shall feel, the more self esteem we shall have, and because we shall then mind another's business less, the fewer will be our conflicts and friction. In this context, "respect" is mutual acknowledgment of defined territorial holdings — recognizing another person's right to certain kinds of territory, not intruding or attacking them, and not entering private space without authorization or permission. When we disagree, we need to be ready to negotiate settlements.

The Individual and the Group

Individual territories are always defined in the context of group claims. In some nations and cultures, individual territories are severely restricted or even nonexistent. Unless there are individual territories, there can be no individual freedom.

The social historian, Orlando Patterson, from Harvard University points out in his book, *Freedom in the Making of Western Culture:*

"For most of human history, and for nearly all of the non-Western world prior to Western contact, freedom was, and for many still remains, anything but an obvious or desirable goal.

"So strong is our commitment to this value, however, and so insistent our claim that this commitment is natural, that we have assumed that something is wrong with the rest of the world and with the majority of human history during which no one ever thought it necessary to express and cherish freedom as an ideal."

Individual freedom and the idea of individual rights are fundamental to us in the United States, perhaps moreso than in any of the other nations of the world. Sometimes, it is carried to the extreme, so that the well being of the larger nation is cast into the background. But, in order for any individual to enjoy personal freedom, it is necessary that individual freedom and group well being are in balance and of equal importance.

History teaches us that many experiments diminishing, or even eliminating, individual freedom (and therefore, individual territory) have been attempted, with similar results.

William Bradford, governor of the Plymouth Colony, made an agreement with the English sponsors of the Pilgrims in 1620, that made all crops, fish and trade goods "common stock," from which the colonists would draw their supplies. This communistic experiment resulted in starvation, confusion and discontent. A drastic change was then made, assigning land to each family, who could keep what they grew on it. Bradford wrote:

"It made all hands very industrious; so much corn was planted than otherwise would have been."

To celebrate, the Pilgrims "set apart a day of thanksgiving."

Another experiment, in the early days of the Kibbutz in Israel, likewise made all property and space group owned and controlled. Individual possessions were not allowed. But, gradually, so many individuals began collecting personal possessions and marking off private space, in violation of the rules, the rules had to be modified.

A similar experiment, on a grander scale, was Soviet Communism. The results were similar to those of the early Pilgrims. It was an economic and group disaster.

These experiments show how fundamental and how powerful the bases are for individual ownership. The strength and productivity of cultures, based on both individual rights *and* group well being are there for all to see in the United States and many nations of the Western world. In such societies it is required of each individual that the rights of others be respected in order to earn the privilege of their reciprocal respect for one's own personal rights. Individual freedom can exist only within the sanction and agreement of the group, and the group has the power, most of the time, to restrict that freedom. We, in the United States, are all fortunate to be living in one of the few nations and cultures that recognizes and gives protection to individual territory and individual freedom.

Index

Index

213

ABOUT THE AUTHORS

Donald Akutagawa, Ph.D.

Donald Akutagawa, Ph.D. is a clinical psychologist in private practice. His work includes evaluation and therapy with individuals, couples and families, as well as the assessment of police and corrections officers candidates. He has authored articles in both technical journals and popular magazines. During his student days at the University of Chicago, he worked under the late Bruno Bettelheim, the noted psychoanalyst. A biographee of *Who's Who*, he is Past President of the Washington Association of Marriage and Family Therapists.

Terry Whitman, Ph.D.

Terry Whitman, Ph.D. is an elementary school counselor in Mill Creek, Washington. He has worked in rural, inner city and suburban school settings. He is a licensed psychologist and a member of the Washington State and American Psychological Associations. Terry's pastimes include lap swimming and roller hockey.

Selected References

ARDREY, Robert. *The Territorial Imperative.* **New York: Dell Publishing Co., Inc., 1966.**
Ardrey's book is a main source of territorial ideas that was meant for the educated general reader in which the basic principles are described and illustrated. Although the situations he deals with are mostly with other animals, he emphasizes the importance of territoriality for humans. This book created quite a sensation when it appeared in 1966.

BAKKER, Cornelius B. and BAKKER-RABDAU, Marianne K. *No Trespassing!* **San Francisco: Chandler and Sharp Publishers, Inc., 1973.**
This book seems to have been written for an academic audience. It is full of detailed concepts about territoriality in humans, and is a good reference for anyone who is interested in delving more deeply into the subject.

HALL, Edward T. *The Hidden Dimension.* **Garden City, New York: Doubleday and Co., Inc., 1966.**
In his book, Hall deals with cultural variations in how people deal with each other and with human territorial behavior. Hall, like Ardrey, brings to the rest of us many scientific observations of a technical nature, and "translates" it into plain English, so it can be understood by the rest of us and put to practical use.

KRUEGER, David W. *Body Self & Psychological Self: A Developmental and Clinical Integration of Disorders of the Self.* **New York: Brunner/Mazel Publishers, 1989.**

This is a technical treatise by a psychiatrist which focuses on the details of the self territory, how it comes into existence, how it develops and how important it is in relation to other people and to external space. It is scholarly, well written and clear in its detailed presentation — a difficult, but eminently worthwhile read.

SOMMERS, Robert. *Personal Space.* **Englewood Cliffs, New Jersey: Prentice-Hall, Inc., 1969.**

This book which was written by an architect, details the application of territorial concepts in architectural structures and functions. Sommers describes the effects such physical forms have on humans. As a group, architects seem to have explored the application of territorial ideas more than most other professions have.